Python Programming for Beginners

The Only Step-by-Step Guide You Need To Learn Python Starting from Zero

Clive Campbell

COPYRIGHT PROTECTED
ProtectMyWork.com
ALL RIGHTS RESERVED

Table of Contents

INTRODUCTION **5**
CHAPTER 1: INTRODUCTION TO PYTHON **6**
PROPERTIES OF PYTHON 6
A BRIEF APPLICATION OF PYTHON 7
WHY YOU SHOULD SELECT PYTHON AS YOUR LANGUAGE 8
Reasons you should consider to write Software Applications using Python *9*
CHAPTER 2: HOW TO INSTALL PYTHON **11**
HOW TO INSTALL PYTHON IN MAC OS X 11
INSTALL AND RUN PYTHON ON LINUX 11
INSTALL PYTHON IN WINDOWS 13
PYTHON INTERACTION 13
CHAPTER 3: PYTHON NUMBERS **19**
INTEGERS AND DECIMAL NUMBERS 19
MATH OPERATORS 19
CHAPTER 4: FUNCTIONS **24**
WHY YOU NEED FUNCTIONS 24
PYTHON FUNCTIONS 24
TYPES OF PYTHON FUNCTIONS 29
CHAPTER 5: PYTHON VARIABLES **36**
ASSIGNMENT OF VARIABLE 36
OBJECT REFERENCES 37
OBJECT IDENTITY 38
CACHE SMALL INTEGER VALUES 38
VARIABLE NAMES 39
RESERVED KEYWORDS 41
CHAPTER 6: OPERATORS AND EXPRESSIONS **42**
ARITHMETIC OPERATORS 43
COMPARISON OPERATORS 44
Equality Comparison-Floating-Point Values *44*
LOGICAL OPERATORS 45
Logical Expressions including Boolean Operands *45*
Computation of Non-Boolean Values in a Boolean Context *46*
CHAPTER 7: PYTHON STRINGS **49**
CREATE AND PRINT STRINGS 49
STRING CONCATENATION 49
REPLICATION OF STRING 50
HOW TO STORE STRING VARIABLES? 50
UPPERCASE AND LOWERCASE STRINGS 50
BOOLEAN METHODS 51

COMPUTING THE LENGTH OF A STRING 51
WHITESPACE 52
Stripping a White Space 52
WORKING WITH STRINGS 52
String Literals 52
Double Quotes 52
Escape Characters 53
Raw Strings 53
Multiline Strings 53
Stripping Strings And Indexes 54

CHAPTER 8: PYTHON TUPLES 56
CHAPTER 9: CONDITIONAL EXECUTION 57

BOOLEAN EXPRESSIONS 57
THE IF STATEMENT 58
THE IF.... ELSE STATEMENT 61
THE PASS STATEMENT 63
FLOATING POINT IN EQUALITY OPERATORS 64
NESTED CONDITIONALS 65
MULTI-DECISION STATEMENTS 66
CONDITIONAL EXPRESSIONS 71
ERRORS FOUND IN CONDITIONAL STATEMENTS 71
THE ADVANCED NATURE OF LOGIC 74

CHAPTER 10: ITERATION 76

WHILE STATEMENT 76
DEFINITE AND INDEFINITE LOOPS 81
THE FOR STATEMENT 82
NESTED LOOPS 84
SUDDEN LOOP TERMINATION 88
BREAK STATEMENT 90
CONTINUE STATEMENT 93
WHILE/ELSE & FOR/ELSE 96
INFINITE LOOPS 98

CHAPTER 11: TIPS TO LEARN PYTHON PROGRAMMING 100

HOW TO MAKE NEW CONCEPTS STICK 100

CONCLUSION 104

Introduction

Python is a commonly used computer language that is general-purpose and versatile. It is very useful as a first computer language because it is brief and easy to read. Python is not as hard to learn as other languages like Java or C++. It is a great language to have in any programmer's stack because it can be used to build many different things, which is why companies such as Yahoo, Red Hat, and Google use it.

You can enhance your resume by learning to code with Python. This language was created to pave the way to write computer code that is easy to understand. Although Python has the same basic format as other languages, it provides additional functionality that simplifies life for a programmer.

This book will teach you the basics of Python as well as show you
Several things we will go over:

- How to make simple patterns for programming, such as loops.
- Learn how to use loops and control lines to make different Python programs.
- Learning about formulas, variables, and operators.
- Study unique data structures such as tuples.
- Learn how to manipulate data, use of break, and continue statements.

The explanations of topics are accompanied by different examples and attempts to emphasize good Python programming practices.

We hope that you will enjoy reading and learning new Python concepts.

Chapter 1: Introduction to Python

Developers who have used Python at one point of their lives will express how fun it was to code with Python. This chapter will introduce the basics of the Python language.

Let's get started!

Python is a language that can be used for a variety of purposes.

This computer language boasts a simple syntax that makes it easier for a new learner of computer coding to understand and use.
The syntax of a language written in Python is clean, and the code is short. The beauty of Python is that it offers you a chance to think more about the task at hand instead of the language syntax.

Some history of Python
Guido van Rossum made Python. Its development began in the 1980s but was first released in February 1991.

Why was Python developed?
The reason why Guido Van Rossum embarked on the move to design a new programming language is that he wanted a computer language that could offer a simple syntax just like the ABC alphabets. This motivation led to the development of a new language named Python.
You may be wondering why name the language Python**?**
First, this language wasn't named after the huge constricting snake called a python. Surprisingly, that's not the origin! One of Rossum's interests was watching comedy series. He was a great fan of the comedy series airing in the late seventies, one of the most famous ones being *Monty Python's Flying Circus*. As a result, the name of the language was borrowed from the titular series.

Properties of Python

- **Easy to learn** – The syntax of Python is simple to understand. Python programmers enjoy writing its syntax more than other languages. Python makes writing code easier and lets the developer focus on the problem instead of the syntax. For someone new to coding, this is a great choice to start your Python career.

- **Portability** – When it comes to Python portability, it offers you the ability to run Python on different platforms without making any changes.
- **Python is described as a high-level language** –You should not be afraid of boring jobs like managing memory and so on. When you run Python code, it changes the language to one that any device you're using can understand, so there is no need to worry about lower-level activities.
- **Object-oriented** – By making objects, Object-Oriented Programming lets you break up a big problem into smaller ones. Being an object-oriented language, Python will allow you to compute solutions for the most difficult problems.
- **Has a huge standard library to compute common tasks** – Python has multiple standard libraries for the programmer to use, so you will not have to write all the lines of code yourself. Instead, you will only import the library of the relevant code.

A Brief Application of Python

Web Applications

Using CMS and tools made in Python, you can build a Web application that can be scalable. Popular environments for developing web applications include Pyramid, Django, Django CMS, and IPhone.

Python is also used to make well-known sites like Instagram, Mozilla Firefox, and Reddit.

Scientific and Numeric Calculations

Many Python tools are made specifically for scientific and numeric calculations. Python is used for general computing tasks. It is also used by libraries like Numpy and Scipy. Some of these libraries are used for certain subjects, like AstroPy for astronomy.

The Python programming language is also used in data mining, machine learning, and deep learning.

A great Language for Tech Programmers

The Python language is an important tool used to demonstrate programming to new programmers and children. It is a great language that has important capabilities and features. It's also one of the easiest languages to understand because of its syntax.

Building Software Prototypes

Python is a good way to make software prototypes. For example, you could make the first version of your game with the Pygame package. If you like the demo, you can choose to make the real game with C++.

Why you should select Python as Your Language

Simple, Beautiful Syntax

Python makes it easier and fun to learn and write a single line of code. The grammar is very understandable. For instance:

- b = 4
- c = 3
- sum = b + c
- print (sum)

Even if it's your first time programming, you can manage to understand the function of this simple program.

Not an Overly Rigid Language

In Python, you don't have to say what kind of variable something is. More so, you don't need to end a line with a semicolon. However, Python demands that you adhere to good practices like the right indentation. These simpler rules simplify learning Python for beginners.

The Language is Expressive

Python will let you write powerful programs that have many functions using fewer lines of code. Once you start to write your own programs, you will be surprised at how much you can do with Python language.

Community and Support

There is a large community of Python developers. You will come across different active online forums, which can be helpful while learning how to program in Python.

Reasons you should consider to write Software Applications using Python

Easy to Read and Maintain

When creating an application, you need to concentrate on the brilliant nature of the source code to make the process of updating and maintaining the code easy. The Python Syntax permits you to demonstrate concepts without writing extra code.
Python also provides the chance to use English terms instead of punctuations. For that reason, one can use Python to build custom applications without writing extra code. When you write code that is easy to read, it simplifies the process of updating the software.

Compatible with Key Platforms and Systems

As said before, Python can run in different operating systems. You can even decide to use Python Interprets to run the code on a defined platform. Additionally, Python is a computer language that is read out loud; you don't have to recompile the code to run it on various platforms. Therefore, you don't need to recompile the code once you make any changes. You can run the altered code without recompiling and confirm the effect of changes done to the code instantly. This feature allows developers to change the code without increasing the building time.

Many Open Source Technologies and Frameworks

Since Python is an open source language, it helps save the cost of the software. You can include different open source Python frameworks, development tools, and libraries to reduce the development time without increasing the cost of development.

Breakdown the Intricate Software Development

You can use Python to build both web and desktop applications, as well as to develop complex scientific programs. Python is designed with properties to support data analysis and visualization. You can use the data analysis properties of Python to build big custom solutions without spending extra energy and time. Alternatively, the data libraries and visualizations provided by Python language allow you to visualize and present data in an approachable and effective way.

Apply Test Driven Development (TDD)

With Python, it is possible to develop a software prototype application very fast. Furthermore, the software application can be developed directly from the prototype by refactoring the python code.

Python simplifies coding and testing through the use of Test Driven Development (TDD) methodology. You can quickly write the relevant tests before writing code and adopting the tests to examine the application code. The tests can also help confirm whether the application fulfills predefined requirements depending on the source code.

Potential Drawbacks

Python has its own drawbacks. For example, it doesn't have built-in features available in other modern programming languages. However, you just need to use Python libraries and frameworks to increase custom software development. Also, Python is slower than other languages like Java and C++. This means you will need to boost the Python application by implementing changes to the application code. Still, you can use Python to simplify software maintenance and speed up the process of software development.

In the end, Python is an extremely useful tool for those looking for easy computer programming or for beginners.

Chapter 2: How to Install Python

In this section, you'll find out how to put Python on your Windows, Linux, or Mac OS X computer.

How to Install Python in Mac OS X

1. Go to Python's main website's Python Download page and click "Download Python" (At the end, there will be a version name.)
2. Open the file after downloading, and start following the directions. When Python finishes the installation, you will see a message that says, "The installation was successful."
3. You should download a good text editor before starting the downloading process. If you are just starting out, you should get Sublime Text, which is free.
4. It's easy to install Sublime Text on your computer. You only need to launch the Sublime Text Disc Image file that you received and proceed in accordance with the guidelines.
5. Once the download is done, open Sublime Text and go to File> New File. Next, give the file a name that ends in ".py," such as "beginner.py" or "hello.py," and save it.
6. Write and save the code. Here's a code to use for beginners:
   Print ("Hello, World!")

"Hello, World!" is printed by a simple program.

7. Go to Tool> Build. Here, you can scroll down to the bottom to see how your program works.

Install and Run Python on Linux

1. First, you need to install the dependencies below.

```
$ sudo apt-get install build-essential checkinstall
$ sudo apt-get install libreadline-gplv2-dev libncursesw5-dev libssl-dev
libsqlite3-dev tk-dev libgdbm-dev libc6-dev libbz2-dev
```

2. Go to the official site's Download Python page and click "Download Python 3.6.0" Don't be afraid to download a different version if you see one. That means there's an updated version.
3. Proceed to the terminal, locate the path where the file has been saved, and then execute the command that is listed below:

$ tar -xvf Python-3.6.0.tgz

This line will get rid of your compressed file. Just know that if you get a different version, the file name will be different. So you should make sure you use the right name for the file.

4. Now shift to the extracted directory.

```
$ cd Python-3.6.0
```

5. To run Python source code on your OS, use these commands.

```
$ ./configure
$ make
$ make install
```

6. It is advised that you install Sublime Text if you are a new beginner. If you are using something else like Ubuntu, then you should run the following commands to install Sublime Text:

```
$ sudo add-apt-repository -y ppa:webupd8team/sublime-text-2
$ sudo apt-get update
$ sudo apt-get install sublime-text
```

7. Start Sublime Text now. Go to File > New File to make a new file.
8. Be sure to save the file with a .py extension, like beginner.py.
9. Write and save the code. Use the following code if you are a beginner:

   print ("Where are you?")

   "Where are you?" will be shown on this programme.
10. Go to the Tool > Build. The result can be seen at the bottom of Sublime Text.

Install Python in Windows

1. Go to the official site's Download Python page and click on Download Python 3.6.0 (or any newer version you see).
2. Once the File has been downloaded, open it and start the startup process. Once the installation of Python is done, IDLE is installed at the same time.
3. Open the IDLE, copy and paste the code below, and press enter.

```
print ("Hello, World!")
```

4. In IDLE, go to File> New Window to make a new file.
5. Afterwards, write a Python code and save it as a .py extension.
6. Go to the module Run > Run and look at the results.

Python Interaction

As said in the first chapter, the Python language is popular because of the level of flexibility and dynamic that a developer can use to achieve different things. Python can be used in real time, such as when you want to try a sentence line by line or learn about new features. It can also be used in script mode to look at all the lines in a file.
Python has the Command Line Window or the IDLE that allows programmers to use it interactively.

Let's look at the command line interaction
The easiest mode to work with Python is through the command line. With this tool, you can see how Python works by seeing how it reacts to each word you type. While it is the fastest way to learn Python, it is not the best. That topic will be covered later.

How to start Python
Depending on what kind of operating system you have on your computer, there are different ways to get to the command line of Python:

- Users of Windows can open the Python command line by clicking on the item in the Start menu. Windows users can also find the folder with a link and press on the Python command line.
- For Linux and Mac OS users, to start a session, you need to open the Terminal Tool and type the Python command.

With computer instructions, you can tell a machine what to do. So, if you want Python to do something, you must type orders that it will understand. Python will then translate the orders into machine-readable code.
To learn to use Python, you will need to print a simple message using the print command:

1. Welcome to Python.

2. Open your Python command line tool.
3. Then, at the >>> prompt, type the following code:
   print ("Welcome to Python!")
4. Press enter to finish creating the code in Python.
5. Next, on the command line window, you'll see the message "Welcome to Python!"

In the above example, Python responded the right way because you typed the correct command in the right format.
Let's say you typed the command incorrectly; then Python will have responded with the following message: Syntax error: Invalid syntax.
When you come across a syntax error message, then know that you have entered an incomplete statement in your code. For example, typing the keyword print in the capital letter (i.e. PRINT) will result in a syntax error.
When you're writing with Python, you don't have to use the print command at all. You can just type your lines between quotes instead. "Welcome to Python!" is an example of this.

How to exit from Python
Once you are done using Python, you can exit by typing the following commands:
Quit ()
Exit ()
Control-Z then press Enter

IDLE: Python's Integrated Development Environment
IDLE stands for "Integrated Development Environment" and is part of the Python software packet. It comes with Python 3, but you can also download third-party IDEs, although they are more complicated. The IDLE tool gives you a safe place to write code and work with Python in a dynamic way. IDLE is in the same area as the icon for the command line. When you press on the button for IDLE, you will be taken to the Python Shell Window.

The Shell is where IDLE starts when you first open it. The Shell is an area that allows you to enter Python code while simultaneously displaying the results of the code in the same session.
When you open the IDLE, it will provide you with a graphical user interface (GUI) that will provide you with all the necessary tools to write, read, and debug your code. One of the advantages of the IDLE is that it will provide the user with different colors to read the code easier and automatic indentation, which is a specific need of Python 3 and newer versions.
If you are working with multiple projects, you will see that the IDLE will also be useful, since it will enable you to manage different projects at the same time, all integrated with the Python framework. This makes it easy for those who are just beginning with the language to see everything in one place and see the results of the code in real time and quickly identify problems.
Note: On your Windows computer, you may start the programme by double-clicking on a Python file. On the other hand, if you right-click on the file, you will find an option labelled "Edit" with IDLE. Launch IDLE, then navigate to the file you want to edit in the File menu to make changes to an existing Python file.

First Python Program

You have already written your first Python program up to this point. In every computer language, the "Hello World Program" is always the first program you write.
We'll look at a different kind of program in the next case. Open IDLE and make a new window to start. If you don't know how to make a new window, just click on "New Window" in the File Menu.
After that, you can type this program:

```
temp = eval(input('Enter a temperature in Celsius: '))
print('In Fahrenheit, that is', 9/5*temp+32)
```

```
temp = eval(input("Enter a temperature in Celsius:"))
print('In Fahrenheit, that is: ', 9/5*temp+32)
```

Navigate to the Run tab in IDLE, and then select the Run Module option. If you don't want to do that, you can avoid doing so by using the F5 key. You will be prompted by the IDLE to save the file, which is something that you should definitely do. Remember to append .py to the end of the file name, since IDLE will not do this for you automatically. The .py extension tells IDLE that the file is a Python program, so it can make the code easier to read by adding colors.

When you have finished saving the file, you can then run it in the shell window. The programme will request the user's temperature at some point. Type the number 20 and press the Enter key. This is how the program will turn out:

```
Enter a temperature in Celsius: 20
In Fahrenheit, that is 68.0
```

```
Enter a temperature in Celsius: 20
In Fahrenheit, that is:  68.0
```

How does the program work? First, type the temperature. The input function requests and records user input. The person sees the part between the quotes. This is defined as a "string," and program users will see it as written in the code. A function that you will not know is "eval"; you will learn more about it when we discuss Python functions. For now, just know it gets numbers.

The next program that you will learn permits you to calculate the number that is the media of two others.

```
num1 = eval(input('Enter the first number: '))
num2 = eval(input('Enter the second number: '))
print('The average of the numbers you entered is', (num1+num2)/2)
```

```
num1 = eval(input("Enter the first number: "))
num2 = eval(input("Enter the second number: "))
print('In Fahrenheit, that is: ', (num1 + num2) / 2)
```

The next thing you will learn about Python is how it works with other things. Spaces elsewhere do not matter. For instance, these lines yield the same result:

```
print('Hello world!')
print ('Hello world!')
print( 'Hello world!' )
```

```
print('Hello World!')
print ('Hello World!')
print( 'Hello World!')
```

Computers automatically follow your commands.

Python uses commas and brackets to understand what is happening. This terminology is hard for the computer to understand, so you must be clear. After a while, placing commas and brackets will feel natural. The Python engine shows you your mistakes so you can fix them.

Accepting input

The entry function makes it easy for users to send information to your program through the program. For instance:

```
name = input('Enter your name: ')
print('Hello, ', name)
```


```
name = input("Enter your name: ")
print('Hello,', name)
```


The standard syntax is:
Variable name = input (message to user)
This structure is used when you want to get a text from a user. However, if you want to get numbers from the user to include in computations, you will have to go an extra mile. Check out this example:

```
num = eval(input('Enter a number: '))
print('Your number squared:', num*num)
```


```
num = eval(input("Enter a number: "))
print('Your number squared: ', num*num)
```


With the "eval" tool, the user's words will be turned into a number. One great thing about this is that you can type phrases like "2*4+9 " and "eval " will figure out what the answer is for you.
Note: When you run a program and it looks like nothing is happening, press the enter option. There is always a glitch with input lines in IDLE.

Printing

Consider the following example:
print ('Hello there')
The inputs to the "print" method should be put in parentheses. In the following program, the word "Hello there" is used as the argument. Everything inside the quotes will be shown exactly as it is written. In the first program shown below, it will print '4+ 2' while the second program will print 8.
print ('4+2')
print (4+ 4)

To display different things at once, you need to use commas to separate the items. However, Python will do it for you and add spaces in between the pieces automatically. For example:

```
print('The value of 3+4 is', 3+4)
print('A', 1, 'XYZ', 2)
```

```
print('The value of 3+4 is', 3+4)
print('A:', 3+4, 'XYZ:', 2)
```

Output

```
The value of 3+4 is 7
A: 7 XYZ: 2
```

Chapter 3: Python Numbers

Integers and Decimal Numbers

Computer chips are designed uniquely. Because of that, integers and decimal numbers have a special representation. The most critical thing to recall is that you only get 15 or so digits of accuracy. It would be great if there were no boundary to the precision but computations happen so fast if you remove the numbers at some point.

When it comes to decimal numbers, the last digit can be left off because computers work in binary and the standard system of numbering for humans is to base 10. This means that if you consider the division of 7/3 in the Python shell, it will display 2.333333333335. This type of operation is defined as a round-off error. In scientific and mathematical computations, this can be a big problem.

Math Operators

This list has common Python operators.

```
+ addition
- subtraction
* multiplication
/ division
** exponentiation
// integer division
% modulo (remainder)
```

Integer division: In general, the integer division will work as the usual division for positive numbers except that it removes the decimal part. For example, 8/5 is 1.6, 8//5 equal to 1. You will learn more about the application of the following operator as you continue to learn Python.

Modulo: This operator % displays the remainder result after division. So if you take 5%3, the result will be 2. The modulo operator is useful when you want to determine if a number is divisible. If the number leaves a remainder of 0, then it is said to be divisible. If not, the number is said not to be divisible.

Another application of the module comes in when you want to set a specific feature in a loop to happen often; to determine that the loop variable modulo 2 is 0. If you obtain yes as the answer, do something different.

In mathematical expressions, the modulo operator is frequently employed. You can "wrap things around" and return to the beginning by using the modulo in your calculation.

Imagine you are playing a game with five other people. Consider a variable player that tracks the active player. It will be player 1's turn once player 5 has completed their turn. The modulo operator is an effective tool for managing this procedure:

```
player = player%5+1
```

```
num_players = 5
current_player = 3

# Determine the next player using the modulo operator
next_player = (current_player + 1) % num_players

print("Current player:", current_player)
print("Next player:", next_player)
```

In this example, num_players represents the total number of players in the game, and current_player represents the player who just completed their turn. We want to use the modulo operator to determine the next player, which should be the player after current_player, or player 4 in this case.

To do this, we add 1 to current_player to get the index of the next player. Then we use the modulo operator to wrap the index around to the start of the player list if we go beyond the last player. Since we have 5 players, the modulo of any number greater than 4 will wrap back to the start of the player list.

In this example, (current_player + 1) % num_players evaluates to (3 + 1) % 5, which is 4. Therefore, the next_player variable is set to 4, which represents player 4 in the game.

The Order of Operations

The order of operations is the list of steps that are taken when operators are run. When you have more than two operators, an order of operations has to be followed. In general, exponentiation is executed first, then multiplication, and then division. Addition and subtraction are the last. The standard math mnemonic is “PEMDAS”, which stands for Parentheses Exponents Multiplication Division Addition Subtraction”. This phrase can be helpful if you are likely to forget.

This also helps when you want to figure out what the average is. Say you have three factors named m, n, and y. You want to find out what the average is.

If you use the expression m+n+y/3, you get a wrong result because the division has higher precedence than addition. Therefore, you need to apply parentheses: (m+n+y)/3.

Note: If you have doubts over something, then proceed and use parentheses. There is no problem when you use parentheses.

Random Numbers

If you want to make your computer game interesting, then you will need to apply the random feature. Python has a module called random. This module will allow you to include random numbers in your program.

First, let's define a module. The Python language comprises math operations, loops, and functions. Everything else is made up of modules. If you need to use a module, you will first need to import. By importing, you will be making Python aware.

Another function is the randint from the random library. Before you can use this function, you will need to write this statement:

```
from random import randint
```

To use the randint function is straightforward: *randint (a, b)* will display a random integer between a and b. For example:

```
from random import randint
x = randint(1,10)
print('A random number between 1 and 10: ', x)

A random number between 1 and 10: 7
```

Every time the program is run, the number will be different.

Functions in Maths

In Python, there is another math module that has familiar math functions such as tan, cos, sqrt, floor, and many more. Also, there are the constants pi, hyperbolic functions, and the inverse trig functions. Check this example:

```
from math import sin, pi
print('Pi is roughly', pi)
print('sin(0) =', sin(0))
Pi is roughly 3.14159265359
sin(0) = 0.0
```

In-built Math Functions

Python has two built-in math functions.

- Abs
- Round

There are two arguments for the round function. The first argument represents the number that should be rounded while the second number is the decimal place that you need to round.

Get Assistance from Python

To learn how to utilize the math module, you can look at the instructions that come with Python. For instance, to execute the following two commands, open the Python shell and type them in:

```
>>> import math
>>> dir(math)
```

Shell Calculator

A great computer can be made with the Python shell. Below is a session example:

```
>>> 23**2
529
>>> s = 0
>>> for n in range(1,10001):
s = s + 1/n**2


1.6448340718480652
>>> from math import *
>>> factorial(10)
3628800
```

A variable is used to store the data. Type the name of the variable and press 'Enter' to find out what it is worth. To figure out what's wrong, you need to look at the factors. If a program does not function properly, you can troubleshoot it by entering the variable names into the shell after the program has finished running and you have determined what the numbers are.

```
>>> s = 1900
>>> s
1900
```

Practice Exercise

1. Develop a computer program that, between the numbers 3 and 6, outputs 50 random integers on the screen.
2. Develop a piece of software that will randomly print numbers between 1 and 10, inclusive.
3. Develop a computer program that requires the user to input two numbers, m and n, and then calculate the average of those values.
4. Design a computer program that will prompt the user to enter the number of seconds, and it will then display the total number of minutes and seconds, i.e.

Chapter 4: Functions

Functions are important in any computer language because they help break up a big program into smaller pieces that are easy to handle. Even if you have to write the same code more than once in your program, functions are still important. Python function blocks start with the word **def**, then the function's name, and then brackets. Any options or settings that you want to pass in should go inside these brackets. Still, you can use these brackets to describe values.

Why You Need Functions

In computer programs, functions control input and output. Programming languages were made so that people could work with data, and functions are the best way to change this kind of data.

A function is the main part of a program's code. Every method is linked to the main code in a way that makes sense. But if a function hasn't been created yet, you'll have to do that before you can use it.

So, you could say that functions are jobs that a person wants to do. But if you define a function once and give it a name, you can use that function again without making the main program look intimidating. This will get rid of lines of code quickly and make it easy to find bugs.

You will learn this later, but for now, remember that you use a function because it can be used more than once. Computer codes are easier to understand because they can be broken down into single jobs that can be run with just one call.

In each computer language, you can make and use functions to do different things with just one call. You are also able to make a variety of calls without always being concerned about how the code fits into the primary code.

Python Functions

Reusability is shown very well by the Python methods. This helps with a wide range of tasks, from building websites to testing. There are different methods that can be used with the Python program. And you can always add other tools to your program that come with ready-to-use features.

All you have to do is download the packages you need and put them into your code to give them the functions you need.

Once a method has been set up, it can be used more than once at any point in the code. Python follows the DRY (Don't Repeat Yourself) idea of software engineering. This concept says that any software patterns that are used more than once should be replaced with abstractions. This is done to avoid redundancy and to make sure that the abstractions can be used easily without revealing any details about how they work.

Being able to use code blocks more than once is a very important part of abstraction in Python. So, to use a function, you only need to know its name, what inputs it takes, what its goal is, if it takes any, and what kind of results it gives if it gives any.

It is the same as operating a car or talking on the phone; you do not need to understand how the components function in order to use them. Instead, it is already configured to serve the most common purposes, which you can put to use right away to accomplish your objectives and spend the rest of your time putting all of the creative elements of your application program into action. As long as a function accomplishes its intended purpose, the details of how it operates on the inside are of little concern to anyone.

Therefore, if you want to use Python, you do not need to know what is going on inside of it until it works the way you want it to. You will still need to be aware of everything that is happening in order to create a new function or modify an existing one. In the same way that you need to understand how an automobile operates before you can build or repair one, the same is true for this. However, once you have created a code that is functional, you will be able to utilize it often without ever having to inspect what is included within it again.

As part of a program, you can call a function that is written once and can be run whenever the program needs it. This lets the code be used again.

A function is part of a program that works with data and gives out results.

In order to construct a Python function, you must preface the function's name with the term "def" and finish the function's definition with brackets and a colon (:).

In Python, rather than using brackets to show blocks, spacing is used. This makes the code easier to understand.

A method in Python can have zero, one, or more than one argument at any given time. A function can have several inputs and produce results when working on variables from other blocks of code or the main programme.

Python functions can either provide back a value or not at all. You can get the value from the execution of the function, or it can be a phrase or value that you highlight after the word "return." Both of these options are valid. When a return line is executed, the program flow reverts to the state it was in immediately prior to the function call, and it continues from that point.

To put it another way, in order to call a Python function from anywhere in your code, all you need to do is reference the function by its name and, if necessary, enclose any arguments in brackets.

The guidelines for giving a variable a name are identical to those for giving a function a name. It might begin with any letter from A to Z, in either lowercase or capital form, or it could begin with an underscore (_). The last name has underscores (_), digits (0-9), and lowercase or capital letters.

1. An identifier might not be chosen from a list of reserved keywords.
2. Using correct language to make the code easier to read.

The easiest way to give a Python method a name is to explain its purpose through the method's title. After the initial line of a function definition, a docstring should be inserted. It is a text that is included in the documentation that explains what the code performs.

Basics of Functions

Functions are vital because they help you avoid the need to write the same code everywhere. In Python, the process of establishing functions is accomplished through the usage of the def line. This statement is finished off with a colon, and the code that will be carried out within the function begins just where the line that defines it leaves off. For instance:

```
def print_hello():
    print('Hello!')

print_hello()
print('1234567')
print_hello()
```

Let's look at this program in detail.
From the following program, the last part of the code has a function call.
If you want to draw a box of stars in your program, a Python function can be helpful. Whenever you want a box, you simply insert the function to draw the box instead of typing different lines of redundant code. Below is the function:

```
def draw_square():
  print('*' * 15)
  print('*', ' '*11, '*')
  print('*', ' '*11, '*')
  print('*' * 15)
```

The advantage of this is that if you want to change the size of the box, all you need to do is adjust the code that is included within the function. This is the only thing you need to do in order to complete this. If, on the other hand, you try to copy and paste the box code everywhere, you will be compelled to edit it wherever you paste it, regardless of where you copied it from.

Arguments

It is possible to pass values to functions in the majority of programming languages. For example:

```
def print_hello(n):
 print('Hello ' * n)
 print()

print_hello(3)
print_hello(5)
times = 2
print_hello(times)
```

The resultant number is preserved in the n variable when the print_hello function is called with the value 3 for one of its parameters. After that, you will be able to reference this variable anywhere in the function's source code.

In Python programming, it is possible to pass a different value to the same function.

```
def multiple_print(string, n)
print(string * n)
print()

multiple_print('Hello', 5)
multiple_print('A', 10)
```

Returning values

Programming is an interesting thing to learn, especially when writing functions. Besides just passing values to functions, you can also create functions that return a result after computation is over.

The following example changes the temperature from Celsius to Fahrenheit.

```
def convert(temp):
  return temp*9/5+32
print(convert(20))
```

A return statement is present in this piece of software, and its job is to relay the results of a computation back to whoever called the function. Remember that the function does not print anything. The printing happens outside the function.
In this case, you can compute the math with the following result:

```
print(convert(20)+5)
```

Python's math module provides access to trigonometric functions, but these functions can only be used with radians. The sine function, which may work with degrees, is as follows.

```
from math import pi, sin
def deg_sin(x):
  return sin(pi * x / 180)
print(deg_sin(20))
```

This is a Python code that defines a function named deg_sin which takes an argument x representing an angle in degrees and returns the sine of that angle in radians. Here's a step-by-step breakdown of what the code does:

1. from math import pi, sin: This line imports two functions from the math module, namely pi (a constant representing the value of π) and sin (a function that returns the sine of an angle in radians).
2. def deg_sin(x): This line defines a function named deg_sin that takes a single argument x.
3. return sin(pi * x / 180): This line calculates the sine of x in radians by converting the angle from degrees to radians using the formula radians = degrees * π / 180, where π is the mathematical constant. The sin() function from the math module is then used to calculate the sine of the angle in radians, and the result is returned.
4. print(deg_sin(20)): This line calls the deg_sin() function with an angle of 20 degrees as the argument and prints the resulting sine value to the console.

So, when this code is executed, it will print the sine value of 20 degrees in radians, which is approximately 0.342.
A function can still return more than one value as a list.

Types of Python Functions

Python Functions fall into many different groups. And each function is different. Here are some examples of different kinds of Python functions:

- Python Recursion Functions
- Python Built-in Functions
- Python user-defined functions
- Python lambda functions

Let us dive deep and learn more about these functions.

Built-in Python Functions

You have a variety of options to choose from while working with the Python interpreter. These kinds of functions are referred to as built-in functions in the industry. For instance, the print () method will display the object either on the standard output device or in the text stream file, depending on which one is specified.

Python 3.6 comes with 68 pre-installed methods to choose from. First, let us take a look at the most important approaches that have been taken so that we can keep things as straightforward as possible.

Python abs () Function

Any number that is entered into this function will have its absolute value returned. If the number is complicated, the value displayed by abs () represents its magnitude.

Syntax

The following is the typical syntax for the abs () function:

Abs (num)

Parameters

The abs () function accepts a single argument:

- **Num**-This is a number whose absolute value should be returned. This number can be:
    a. Integer
    b. Complex number
    c. Floating number

Example

```
# random integer
integer = -20
print('Absolute value of -20 is:', abs(integer))

#random floating number
floating = -30.33
print('Absolute value of -30.33 is:', abs(floating))
```

Python all () function

If every element in a particular iterable is true, then the all () method will return True as its result. In that case, it will show the value False.

Syntax

The syntax of each and every () method is as follows:
all (iterable)

Parameters

The all () method only takes one parameter to work with:

- Iterable- Any iterable (tuple, list, dictionary, etc.) which has the elements.

For example:

```
# all values true
l = [1, 3, 4, 5]
print(all(l))

# all values false
l = [0, False]
print(all(l))

# one false value
l = [1, 3, 4, 0]
print(all(l))

# one true value
l = [0, False, 5]
print(all(l))

# empty iterable
l = []
print(all(l))

Output

True
False
False
False
True
```

Python ascii () Function

The string that contains a representation of an object that may be printed will be returned by this method. It will bypass any non-ASCII characters that are contained within the string by utilizing the u, x, or U escapes.

Syntax

The following is the syntax for the asci () method:
ascii (object)

Parameters

The asci method is able to process objects such as lists, strings, and others.

Example

```
normalText = 'Python is interesting'
print(ascii(normalText))

otherText = 'Pythön is interesting'
print(ascii(otherText))

print('Pythn is interesting')

Output

'Python is interesting'
'Pythn is interesting'
Pythön is interesting
```

Python bin () function

The bin function converts an integer into its corresponding binary string and returns that string. In the event that the parameter is not an integer, it is necessary to utilize the _index_ () method in order to process an integer.
The following is an example of the syntax for a bin method: bin (num)
The bin () method only takes one parameter to work with:

- Num-This is an integer number whose binary equivalent has to be computed. If not an integer, it has to run the _index_ () method to output an integer.

```
number = 5
print('The binary equivalent of 5 is:', bin(number))

Output

The binary equivalent of 5 is: 0b101
```

Python bool () function

The value of an integer can be converted into its corresponding binary string using the bool () method, which then returns that string. In order to display an integer, it is necessary to use the __index__ () function if the parameter in question is not an integer.
The syntax for the bool () method is as follows:
Bool([value])

Parameters
It is not a must to pass a value to bool (). If you don't pass a value, bool () returns a False value.
Overall, bool () accepts a single parameter value.

Example:

```
test = []
print(test,'is',bool(test))

test = [0]
print(test,'is',bool(test))

test = 0.0
print(test,'is',bool(test))

test = None
print(test,'is',bool(test))

test = True
print(test,'is',bool(test))

test = 'Easy string'
print(test,'is',bool(test))

Output

[] is False
[0] is True
0.0 is False
None is False
True is True
Easy string is True
```

Python Recursive functions
In Python programming, a function can reference another function. Also, functions don't have to be called by other functions, but instead it can call itself.
An example of a recursive function is one to find the factorial of numbers. 6 factorial means 1*2*3*4*5*6= 720

Example:

```
# An example of a recursive function to
# find the factorial of a number

def calc_factorial(x):
    <em>"""This is a recursive function
    to find the factorial of an integer"""

    </em>if x == 1:
        return 1
    else:
        return (x * calc_factorial(x-1))

num = 4
print("The factorial of", num, "is", calc_factorial(num))
```

In this example, calc_factorial () is a recursive function.

Pros recursion

1. A recursive function improves the appearance of code. The code looks elegant and clean.
2. A difficult problem is divided into small parts using recursion

Cons of recursion

1. Recursive calls consume a lot of time and memory.
2. Sometimes the logic of recursion is difficult to follow.

Python Lambda Functions

A function without a name is referred to as an anonymous function. The lambda keyword denotes anonymous.

Using Lambda functions in Python

The syntax of python lambda function includes:
Lambda arguments: expression

Example:

```
# Program to show the use of lambda functions

double = lambda x: x * 2

# Output: 10
print(double(5))

10

In [1]:
```

Python user-defined functions

As the name suggests, user-defined functions refer to functions defined by the user.

Pros of user-defined functions

1. User-defined functions assist in the sub-dividing a huge program into small parts.
2. If a program has a block of code that is executed multiple times, the function can include those blocks of code and run them when the calling function needs it.
3. Programmers working on large projects might break up their labor by computing a variety of different functions to divide the workload.

Syntax

```
def function_name(argument1, argument2, ...) :
        statement_1
        statement_2
        ....
```

In conclusion, the ideas that have been discussed in this chapter are intended to be of assistance to you in the process of developing your own Python functions by adding operability and functionality to the same.

When you are attempting to construct an application, this will come in handy because it will simplify the process and allow you to tailor it to your specific requirements. Now, in order to easily create applications, you need to have the ability to use Python functions.

Chapter 5: Python Variables

If you plan to write complex code, then you must include data that will change the execution of the program.
That is what you are going to learn in this chapter. At the end of the chapter, you will learn how the abstract object term can explain each section of data in Python and also how to change objects with the help of variables.
Variables in Python programming are the data types in Python as the name implies. In the programming world, variables are memory locations where you store a value. The value that you store might change in the future depending on the descriptions.
In Python, a variable is created once a value is assigned to it. It doesn't need any extra commands to declare a variable in Python. There are specific rules and guidelines to adhere to while writing a variable.

Assignment of Variable

Look at variables as a name linked to a specific object. When you are programming in Python, you do not need to declare variables before using them, as is the case with other programming languages. Instead, you give a value to a variable, and then you start using that variable straight away.. The assignment occurs using a single equals sign (=):
Y= 100
The same way a literal value can be shown from the interpreter using a REPL session, so it is to a variable:
Later if you assign a new value to Y and use it again, the new value is replaced.
Python has room for chained assignments. You are able to assign the same value to several separate variables all at the same time.
Example:

```
>>> a = b = c = 300
>>> print(a, b, c)
300 300 300
```

This chained assignment allocates 300 to the three variables simultaneously. Most variables in other programming languages are statically typed. This means that a variable is always declared to hold a given data type. Now any value that is assigned to this variable should be similar to the data type of the variable.

However, variables in Python don't follow this pattern. In fact, a variable can hold a value featuring a different data type and later be reassigned to hold another type.

Object References

What really happens when you assign a variable?
This is a vital question in Python programming because it is different from what goes on in other languages.
First, Python is an object-oriented language. In fact, each data item in Python is an object of a given type.
Consider the following example:

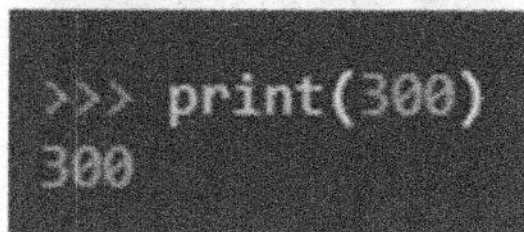

When the interpreter comes across the statement print (300), the following takes place:

- Assigning it the value 300.
- Builds an integer object.
- Outputs it to the console.

Example

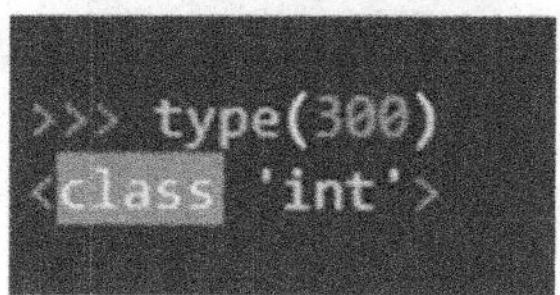

The symbolic name that can be used as a pointer to an object in Python is referred to as a variable. A name can be used to refer to an object that has had a variable allocated to it after the variable has been assigned to the object. On the other hand, the data itself is contained inside of the object.
The life of an object starts once it is created; at this point, the object may have one reference. In the lifetime of an object, other references to the object can be created. An object will remain active as long as it has one reference.
But when the number of references to the object drops to zero, it cannot be accessed again. The lifetime of the object is then said to be over. Python will finally realize that it is inaccessible and take the allocated space so that it can be used for something different. This process is called garbage collection.

Object Identity

Every object created in Python is assigned a number to identify it. In other words, there is no point where two objects will share the same identifier during a time when the lifetimes of the object overlap. When the count of an object reference drops to zero and it is garbage collected, then the identifying number of the object is reclaimed to be used again.

```
>>> n = 300
>>> m = n
>>> id(n)
60127840
>>> id(m)
60127840

>>> m = 400
>>> id(m)
60127872
```

Cache Small Integer Values

From your knowledge of the variable assignment and referencing of variables in Python, you will not be surprised by:

```
>>> m = 300
>>> n = 300
>>> id(m)
60062304
>>> id(n)
60062896
```

In this code, Python defines the object of integer type using the value 300 and allows m to refer to it. Similarly, n is allocated to an integer object using the value 300 but not with a different object. Let us consider the following:

```
>>> m = 30
>>> n = 30
>>> id(m)
1405569120
>>> id(n)
1405569120
```

In this example, both m and n have been separately allocated to integer objects holding the value 30. But in this instance, id (m) and id (n) are similar.
The interpreter will develop objects between [-5, 256] at the start, and later reuse it. Therefore, if you assign unique variables to an integer value, it will point to the same object.

Variable Names

The previous examples have used short variables like m and n. But you can still create variable names with long words. This really helps to explain the use of the variable when a user sees the variable.
In general, Python variable names can be of any length and can have uppercase and lowercase letters. Also, the variable names can include digits from 0-9 and the underscore character. Another restriction is that the first character of a variable cannot be an integer. For instance, all these are important variable names:

```
>>> name = "Bob"
>>> Age = 54
>>> has_W2 = True
>>> print(name, Age, has_W2)
Bob 54 True
```

Since a variable cannot start with a digit, this program will show the following result:

```
>>> 1099_filed = False
  1099_filed = False
      ^
SyntaxError: invalid decimal literal
```

Keep in mind too that lowercase letters and uppercase letters are different. Using the underscore character is important as well:

```
>>> age = 1
>>> Age = 2
>>> aGe = 3
>>> AGE = 4
>>> a_g_e = 5
>>> _age = 6
>>> age_ = 7
>>> _AGE_ = 8

>>> print(age, Age, aGe, AGE, a_g_e, _age, age_, _AGE_)
1 2 3 4 5 6 7 8
```

Nothing will prevent you from defining two variables in the same program that have names like number and Number. However, this is not advised at all. It would definitely confuse anyone going through your code, and even yourself, after you have stayed for a while without looking at the code.

It is important to assign descriptive variable names to make it clear on what it is being used for. For instance, say you are determining the number of people who have graduated from college. You may choose any of the following:

```
>>> numberofcollegegraduates = 2500
>>> NUMBEROFCOLLEGEGRADUATES = 2500
>>> numberOfCollegeGraduates = 2500
>>> NumberOfCollegeGraduates = 2500
>>> number_of_college_graduates = 2500

>>> print(numberofcollegegraduates, NUMBEROFCOLLEGEGRADUATES,
... numberOfCollegeGraduates, NumberOfCollegeGraduates,
... number_of_college_graduates)
2500 2500 2500 2500 2500
```

All are great choices than n, or any other variable. At least you can understand from the name the value of the variable.

Reserved Keywords

There is one limit on identifiers names. The Python language has a unique set of keywords that defines specific language functionality. No object can use the same name as a reserved keyword.

Python Keywords

False	def	if	raise
None	del	import	return
True	elif	in	try
and	else	is	while
as	except	lambda	with
assert	finally	nonlocal	yield
break	for	not	
class	from	or	
continue	global	pass	

You can see reserved words in python by typing help ("keywords") on the Python interpreter. Reserved keywords are case-sensitive. So you should never change them but use them exactly as they appear. All of them are in lowercase, except for the following: True, False, and None.
If you attempt to create a variable using a reserved word, it will result in an error.

Chapter 6: Operators and Expressions

In the last chapter, we looked at Python variables. We hope that you now understand how to define and name Python objects well.

Let's do some work with them.

First, we'll look at operators in Python:

The term "operator" refers to a specific symbol in Python that stands for a particular operation. Operands are the numbers that the operator works on.

See this example:

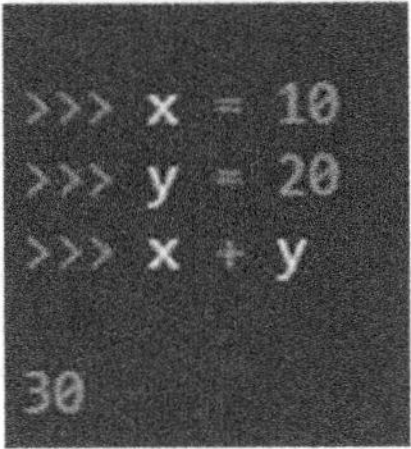

```
>>> x = 10
>>> y = 20
>>> x + y

30
```

In this instance, x and y are combined by the use of the + operator. Operands can be literal values or variables pointing to objects. A literal value is the most common type of operand.

An expression is a group of operators like x + y - z. There are many ways to mix data items in Python to make expressions. Here are some examples:

Arithmetic Operators

Arithmetic operators include +, -, **, //, %, and /.
An example to show some of these operators in a program include:

```
>>> a = 4
>>> b = 3
>>> +a
4
>>> -b
-3
>>> a + b
7
>>> a - b
1
>>> a * b
12
>>> a / b
1.3333333333333333
>>> a % b
1
>>> a ** b
64
```

The outcome of a standard division (/) is a float even when the yield is equally divided by the divisor.
The fractional part has been removed, leaving only the integer part, if the outcome of a floor division (//) is positive. The next smallest integer must be rounded when the output is negative:

```
>>> a = 4
>>> b = 3
>>> +a
4
>>> -b
-3
>>> a + b
7
>>> a - b
1
>>> a * b
12
>>> a / b
1.3333333333333333
>>> a % b
1
>>> a ** b
64
```

Comparison Operators

These operators include ==, <=, >,!=, < and >=. Examples of comparison operators include:

```
>>> a = 10
>>> b = 20
>>> a == b
False
>>> a != b
True
>>> a <= b
True
>>> a >= b
False

>>> a = 30
>>> b = 30
>>> a == b
True
>>> a <= b
True
>>> a >= b
True
```

In Boolean settings like conditional and loop lines, comparison operators control program behavior.

Equality Comparison-Floating-Point Values

The numbers that are saved inside a floating object may not be what you think they can be. So, it's a waste of time to compare floating-point values to see if they are exactly the same. Take, for example:

```
>>> x = 1.1 + 2.2
>>> x == 3.3
False
```

The inner representation of addition operands doesn't reflect exactly to 1.1 and 2.2, and thus you cannot depend on x to make a comparison to 3.3.
The best way to determine if two floating-point values are "equal" is to compare their nearness. For example:

```
>>> tolerance = 0.00001
>>> x = 1.1 + 2.2
>>> abs(x - 3.3) < tolerance
True
```

abs () displays an absolute value. If the absolute values of the two integers are within a tolerance, they are almost comparable.

Logical Operators

Logic operators like or, not, and, "and" change and join Boolean formulas to do more complicated calculations.

Logical Expressions including Boolean Operands

In Python, there are some objects and functions that are of the Boolean type. In other words, they are the same as either the False or True Python objects. Among other things:

When the operands are Boolean, it is easy to explain logical formulas that use or, not, and "and."

See how they work in a program:

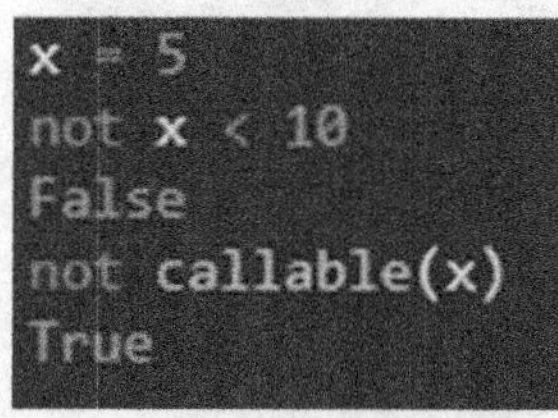

```
x = 5
not x < 10
False
not callable(x)
True
```

Operand	Value	Logical Expression	Value
x < 10	True	not x < 10	False
Callable (x)	False	not callable (x)	True

Computation of Non-Boolean Values in a Boolean Context

Most statements and things don't have a True or False equivalent. Even so, they can't be said to be "false" or "true" in a Boolean setting.
So, what's real and what's not?
This is considered false in Python when it is used in a Boolean context:

- The Boolean value is False.
- An empty string.
- The unique value that Python's None term represents.
- Any number that is zero.

Almost all other things that can be created in Python are thought to be true.
With the built-in bool () method, you can find out if a statement or object is "true." If the argument is true, bool () gives True, and if it is false, it returns False.

```
# Define some objects with different truth values
empty_string = ""
non_empty_string = "hello"
zero_number = 0
non_zero_number = 42
none_value = None
list_value = []
dict_value = {}

# Use the bool() function to determine the truthiness of each object
print(bool(empty_string)) # False
print(bool(non_empty_string)) # True
print(bool(zero_number)) # False
print(bool(non_zero_number)) # True
print(bool(none_value)) # False
print(bool(list_value)) # False
print(bool(dict_value)) # False
```

The Built-in Composite Data Object

Dict, set, tuple, and list are some of the built-in composite data types available in Python. These are what might be called "container" type data, hosting other items. When an object of this type is empty or true when it is not empty, it is said to be false.

Logical Expressions that Include Non-Boolean Operands

"And, or, and not" modify and combine non-Boolean values. Operand "truthiness" impacts the result.

"not" **and Non-Boolean Operands**

The following is what happens for non-Boolean value x:

If x is	not x is
"truthy"	False
"falsy"	True

Some more complex examples:

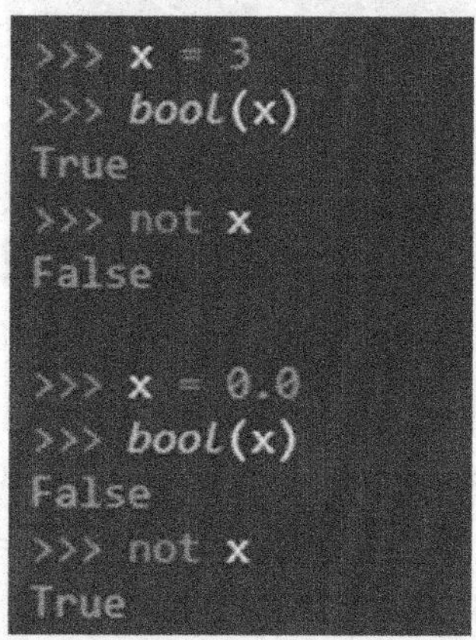

```
>>> x = 3
>>> bool(x)
True
>>> not x
False

>>> x = 0.0
>>> bool(x)
False
>>> not x
True
```

Compound Logical Expressions and Short-Circuit Evaluation

You have currently encountered expressions with a single or OR operator and two operands:

a or b

a and b

Compound logical expressions can be created by combining multiple logical operands and operators.

The Compound "Or" Expressions

Take a look at this expression:

```
x1 or x2 or x3 or … xn
```

This statement is true if one of the xi is true.
This statement employs a technique known as "short-circuit evaluation" in Python. The xi operands are processed sequentially from left to right. The entire sentence is assumed to be true once its veracity has been established. At this moment, Python terminates and no additional terms are discovered. The value of the entire statement is represented by the xi at the conclusion of the test.
The visual representation of a short-circuit review is shown here. Say you have a straightforward "identity" function called f () that performs the following:

- F () accepts a single argument
- It outputs the argument to the console
- It returns the argument passed to it as the return value.

For example:

```
>>> f(0)
-> f(0) = 0
0

>>> f(False)
-> f(False) = False
False

>>> f(1.5)
-> f(1.5) = 1.5
1.5
```

Since f () returns the argument that was supplied to it, it is possible to define the value of arg that determines whether the expression is true or false. Additionally, f () outputs its argument to the console, demonstrating whether it was called or not.
Look at the compound logical expression that follows:

```
>>> f(0) or f(False) or f(1) or f(2) or f(3)
-> f(0) = 0
-> f(False) = False
-> f(1) = 1
1
```

First, f(0) will be determined by the Python interpreter; the outcome is 0. 0 is a false value in mathematics. The computation moves from left to right since this expression is not yet true. False will be the result of the next operand, f (False). This is also untrue, and the analysis goes on.

Chapter 7: Python Strings

A string data type is the main unit of programming. A string can be a constant or a variable. Strings consist of more than one character.

Create and Print Strings

Strings are surrounded by either single quotes (‘) or double quotes (“). For that reason, to define a string, you need to enclose it with single or double quotes.
For example:
“The first program.”
‘Second program.’
It is up to you to decide if you want to use single or double quotes. The only thing you need to ensure is that you become consistent.

String Concatenation

String concatenation is joining strings to create a new string. The + operator is useful when you want to perform string concatenation. Don’t forget that if you use numbers, the + operator becomes an addition operator.
Example of how to concatenate strings:

```
print ('Come' + 'Back to school')
```

Still, you can place whitespace between strings.
When it comes to string concatenation, avoid using the + operator with diverse data types.
For example:
print ('First program' + 34)
This will output an error message.
But if you want to create a string like “feel23”, you can do so by enclosing the number 23 in quotes. This will make it a string instead of an integer. Changing numbers into strings for concatenation is important when working with zip codes.
If you combine more than one string, you get a new string to use in the whole program.

Replication of String

Situations occur that demand the use of Python to automate functions and one way to do this is by repeating a string multiple times. You can accomplish this with the * operator. The * operator does a different function if used with numbers.

When you use it with a single string and integer, the * becomes the string replication operator. It will repeat a single string different times you want via the integer you offer.

For instance: This code will print the name Python 7 times without typing 7 times:

print ("Python" * 7)

Using string replication, you can repeat a different string times you want.

How to Store String Variables?

Variables refer to symbols which one can hold data in a program. Think of variables as empty boxes that you enter data or value. As said before, strings are data, and you can use them to take the space of variables. Declaring a string as a variable can simplify the process of using strings in the whole of Python programs.

To keep a string within a variable, you need to allocate a variable to a string. For example:

My_string = "My son likes Pizza."

My_string is a variable. Now you can proceed to print My_string which stores the data in string format.

print(My_string)

This will output the result: My son likes Pizza.

Using variables in place of strings eliminates the need to retype a string every time you want to use it. This simplifies the process of coding and makes it easy to manipulate strings inside a program.

Uppercase and Lowercase Strings

In the strings functions, the str.upper () and str.lower () functions change all the letters in a string so that they are all capital letters or all lower-case letters. Since strings are "immutable," these functions create a new string.

Let us change the string "Wake up" to become upper case:

my_string = "wake up"

print(my_string.upper())

Output

WAKE UP

Next, let us change the string to lowercase:

print(my_string.lower())
Output
wake up
The two string methods, str.upper() and str.lower(), make evaluating and comparing strings easier by keeping the case the same. So, even if a person writes their name in small letters, you can still tell if it is in the database by looking at all-caps names.

Boolean Methods

Python is made up of string methods that are used to figure out the meaning of a Boolean. When you want to make forms for people to fill out, these methods are important. If we are asking for a postal code, you should only accept a string of numbers.
It is important to check whether characters are all capital letters, all title cases, or all lower cases because it makes sorting data easier. It also makes it possible to organize the data gathered by collecting and changing strings.
When you want to check if something a user types matches a certain value, you need to use the Boolean string functions.

Computing the Length Of A String

The len () function counts how many characters there are in a string. This method is very important if you want to set a minimum or maximum length for passwords. For example, to shorten longer strings to fit within certain limits so they can be used in abbreviations. To show how this works, you will figure out how long a string of sentences is:

```
open_source = "Sammy contributes to open source."
print(len(open_source))

Output
33
```

In this case, the open_source variable has been configured to be equal to the string, which is then given to the len() method by using len(open_source). The method is then given to print (), which indicates to the computer what to show on the screen.
Remember that character, even if it is surrounded by single or double marks or blank characters. The len() method will be used to count these.
Python's str.split(), str.join(), and str.replace () functions can also be used to change text.

The str.join() function joins two strings but in a method in which it passes one string to another.

Whitespace

These are characters which the computer knows but readers cannot see. The most common type of whitespace is newlines, spaces, and tabs.
It is easy to create space because you have been using it since the time you have used computers. Newlines and tabs represent unique character combinations.
You can use tabs anyplace you want in a string.
The character combination for tabs is "\t" while a new line is represented by "\n."

Stripping a White Space

In most instances, you will let users type text into a box, and then read the text and use it. It is simple for people to apply extra whitespace at the start or end of their text.
In general, it is good to remove this whitespace from strings before you begin to work with them.

Working with Strings

String Literals

Including string values in a Python code is an easy thing. It starts and ends with a single quote. But the question is, how can you apply a quote inside a string? If you type "That is Mark's car." It will not work because Python considers the end of the string as Mark and the remaining section is invalid. Luckily, strings can be entered in many ways.

Double Quotes

Like single quotes, double quotes can be used to begin and end strings. However, the advantage of double quotes is that a single quote character can be included in the string.
Enter the next line of code into the interactive Python shell:
>>> spam = "That is Mark's cat."
Python recognizes that a single quote is a part of the string and does not finish it because a string always begins with a double quote. However, if you want to use both single and double quotes in a string, you will need to use escape characters.

Escape Characters

With the help of an escape character, you can add characters that are hard to put into a string. A backslash and the character you want to add to the string make up an escape character. Even though there are two characters, it is still called a single escape character. For example, for a single quote, the escape character is \'. This character can be part of a string that begins and ends with a single quote. To learn how escape characters operate, type this code into the Python shell:

```
>>> spam = 'Say hello to Bob\'s mother.'
```

Python can tell from the backslash in Bob\'s single quote that this single quote is not the end of the string value. You can use single quotes and double quotes in your strings with the escape characters \' and \".

Raw Strings

You can make a raw string by putting r before the first quote mark in a string. All escape marks will be removed from a raw string, and any backslashes will be shown. For example:

```
>>> print(r'That is Joyce\'s car.')
That is Joyce\'s car.
```

Since this is a raw string, Python uses the backslash as a component of the string, not as the start of an escape character. Raw strings are useful if you type string values that have numerous backslashes like the strings applied for regular expressions.

Multiline Strings

It is simple to combine strings with other strings, even though you can add a new line to a string by using the \n escape character. A multiline string in Python must begin and conclude with either three single or triple quotes. It is possible to consider any tabs, quotes, or newlines in between the "triple quotes" to be a part of the string. Inside a multiline string, the Python indentation rules do not apply.

Type the following in your file editor:

```
print('''Dear Alice,

Eve's cat has been arrested for catnapping, cat burglary, and extortion.

Sincerely,
Bob''')
```

If you run this code, you will get the following result:

```
Dear Alice,

Eve's cat has been arrested for catnapping, cat burglary, and extortion.

Sincerely,
Bob
```

Keep in mind that a single quote character in the word *Eve's* doesn't have to be escaped. In a raw string, you do not have to escape single or double quotes. A call print () would show the same text, but it does not work with a string multiline.

Multiline Comments

Even if the hash character marks the beginning of a comment on the next line, comments that span more than one line always use a multiline string. Below is a genuine Python code:

```
"""This is a test Python program.
Written by Al Sweigart al@inventwithpython.com

This program was designed for Python 3, not Python 2.
"""

def spam():
    """This is a multiline comment to help
    explain what the spam() function does."""
    print('Hello!')
```

Stripping Strings And Indexes

Think of a string like "Hello world!" as a list, where each word is an item with a corresponding number.

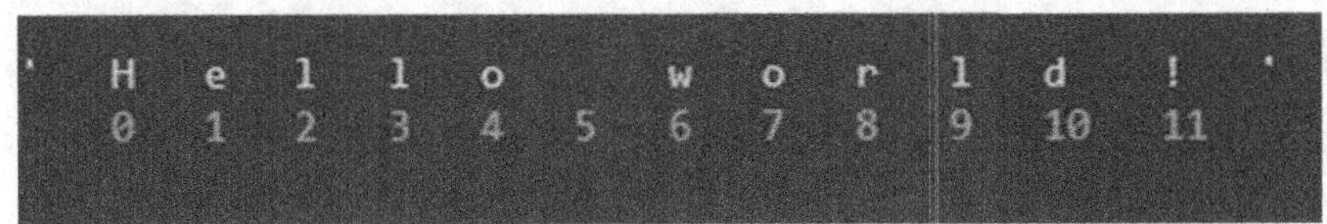

In this example, space and the exclamation mark are also counted. This gives you a total of 12.

Enter the following code:

```
>>> spam = 'Hello world!'
>>> spam[0]
'H'
>>> spam[4]
'o'
>>> spam[-1]
'!'
>>> spam[0:5]
'Hello'
>>> spam[:5]
'Hello'
>>> spam[6:]
'world!'
```

Directly addressing an index gives you a character stored in that point. If you apply a range, the starting index must be counted, too.
Something else that you must remember is that slicing a string doesn't change the beginning of the string.
You can retain a slice from a certain variable in a separate variable. Try to enter the following into the interactive shell.

```
>>> spam = 'Hello world!'
>>> fizz = spam[0:5]
>>> fizz
'Hello'
```

Chapter 8: Python Tuples

Tuples are like data sequences with some little difference to lists. Tuples are immutable; you cannot change, modify, or delete the elements. The syntax that affirms it is a tuple instead of a list is that the elements of a tuple are positioned inside parentheses and not brackets.

The tuple is the default type of sequence in Python. Thus, if I arrange three values here, the computer will consider the new variable as a tuple. Still, we can say the three values will be organized into a tuple. For the same reason, you can allocate various values to the same number of variables.

The same way it can be done for lists, it is possible to index values by specifying their position inside the brackets.

Additionally, you can still include Python tuples inside the lists. Then, every tuple becomes a different element inside the list.

Python tuples resemble lists but there are small differences that you don't need to overlook.

They can be significant when you handle various comma separated values. For example, if you set age and years of school as variables, and you have the correct numbers in a string format, separated by a comma. The split method with the correct indication inside the parentheses will allocate 30 as the value for age and 17 as the number of years in school. We can output the two variables separately to verify the result.

Everything looks correct—great!

Finally, functions can generate tuples in the form of return values. This is important because a function can only display a single tuple having multiple values.

Chapter 9: Conditional Execution

Most of the program examples used so far run the same statements no matter the input entered. The vast majority of programs follow a linear procedure in which statement1 is executed first, followed by statement2 and statement3, and so on, right up until the very last statement, at which point the program terminates.. This chapter will look at program features that allow optional execution of statements.

Boolean Expressions

Also known as a predicate, these expressions may include at least one possible value. The name Boolean originates from George Boole—a British mathematician. If you study discrete mathematics, you will learn more about Boolean algebra, which focuses on logical expressions operations. Even though they may seem limiting when compared to number expressions, Boolean expressions can be used to make interesting programs.
As we have already said, True and False are both Boolean statements in the Python language. The bool class is what Python's Boolean statements look like in the Python shell. You already know that False and True are the only two parts of a simple Boolean statement. A comparison of two number expressions to see if they are the same or different is still a Boolean expression. Relational operators are used to compare two expressions in the simplest Boolean expressions. The simplest type of Boolean expression involves relational operators to make a comparison of two expressions.
Expressions such as 5 < 10 are valid but of little significance because 5 is always less than 10. The True expression is simple and less likely to bring confusion among readers. Since it is possible for variables to get new values at the time of program execution, Boolean expressions are relevant when the true values depend on values of one or more variables.

```
>>> x = 10
>>> x
10
>>> x < 10
False
>>> x <= 10
True
>>> x == 10
True
>>> x >= 10
True
>>> x > 10
False
>>> x < 100
True
>>> x < 5
False
```

The initial input gives the value 10 to the variable x. The relation operators are put to the test in the other statements.

The If Statement

"If" is a python keyword that indicates the start of the statement.
The condition has the expression that will determine if the body is executed. It is important to include a colon immediately after the condition. Sometimes, you may think that the Boolean expressions previously discussed are of little use in practical scenarios. However, Booleans are significant for a program to adjust its behavior at the time of execution. In most practical and useful programs, it is hard for Boolean expressions to miss.
Execution errors in programming emerge because of logic errors. One way these mistakes can happen is if you input Zero for the divider. Programmers have the ability to take significant measures to eliminate the possibility of division by zero.

```
print('Please enter two numbers to divide.')
dividend = int(input('Please enter the first number to divide: '))
divisor = int(input('Please enter the second number to divide: '))
# If possible, divide them and report the result
if divisor != 0:
print(dividend, '/', divisor, "=", dividend/divisor)
```

In the above program, the print statement may not run based on what the user types. For instance: If a person puts Zero for the second number, the program will do the following. It will print nothing after the value is entered:

```
Please enter two numbers to divide.
Please enter the first number to divide: 32
Please enter the second number to divide: 0
```

The last line of code in this program starts with the if statement. In other words, it is not a must for this statement to execute the code inside it. The if statement in the following example will only do an analysis of the print function if the current value of the variable divisor is not equal to zero.

Therefore, the formula Boolean is: divisor!= 0
This expression tells the computer whether or not to run the line in the if block. If the fraction is not zero, the warning is shown by the program. If not, nothing will come out of the computer after the entry.
The standard format for if the statement is as follows:

```
If (condition):

Block
```

The block includes statements to be executed. It is necessary to indent statements inside the block.

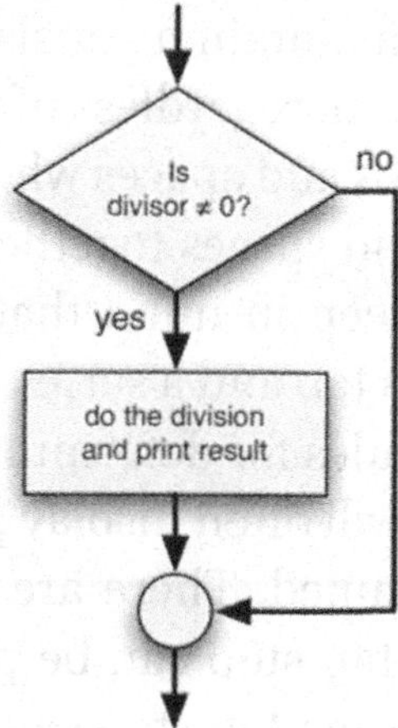

A sufficient amount of whitespace is required between the if statement and the line that initiates the if statement. Technically speaking, the block is a component of the if sentence. The "body" of the if statement is another name for this part of the statement. Because of the way the rules are designed to work in Python, the block always needs to be indented. Some Python developers put the statement on the same line as the if when the block only has one statement. For example:

```
if x < 10:
y = x
```

This can be rewritten as:

```
if x < 10: y = x
```

But it cannot be written as:

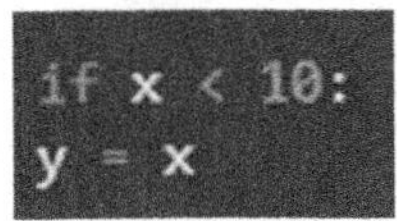

Because the processing of the assignment line is hidden when there is no indentation. Indentation describes the way Python decides the statement that should be part of the block.

What is the count of spaces to indent? Python rules require at least one but other Python developers use two while four is the most popular. However, those who like a dramatic display apply eight. If you are lost on whether to use one, two, four, or eight, then we advise you to apply the recommended four spaces by Python style.

You can eliminate the need to manually count the number of spaces between words by using the Tab key, which is supported by the vast majority of text tools available on computers. You are required to maintain a consistent indentation distance throughout the entirety of your Python program, regardless of which indentation distance you select. Make sure that you do not mix tabs and spaces when you are indenting statements inside of a block. You cannot use tabs and spaces together for indenting in Python 3. You must choose one or the other. Also, keep in mind that the majority of text editors make it difficult to differentiate between a tab and a series of spaces, so keep that in mind as well.

When using various editors, the rules for determining how many spaces are equivalent to a tab can vary greatly. A tab stop will often display a distance from the left edge of the text window that has been predetermined. There are multiple tab stops available in many editors. For instance, the initial tab stop can be placed eight characters away from the start of the line, and each succeeding tab stop can be placed eight characters away from the one that came before it.

The user is only allowed to adjust the settings for the location of the tab stops in the majority of editors. When you press the tab key in the editor, the cursor can advance to the next available tab and then stop somewhere inside the line. On the other hand, using the space bar will consistently bring the pointer one letter further to the right.

You might try using one editor to create a Python file and then opening that file in another editor that uses different tab stops. Lines that were exactly indented out in the previous editor would be misplaced in the new one since it uses a different formatting system. In one editor, putting four spaces between lines of code would result in the same appearance as in the other editor, which would have the same appearance.

Tabs can be used instead of spaces for indenting code in Python version 3. However, you are unable to combine both of them into a single source file because of the spaces. When the Tab key is tapped, the majority of text editors have a setting that automatically replaces a certain amount of spaces with tabs.

The concept of true and false in Python extends beyond what we typically think of as Boolean statements, which is a benefit for those who write in Python. For example:

```
if 1:
  print('one')
```

This statement will print one. But the statement:

```
if 0:
  print('zero')
```

Will not print anything. The reason is that the integer value zero is considered to be false by Python. Also, the floating point 0.0 is considered false but other floating point values are considered to be true. A false string is also an empty string, like '' or ''. A true string is one that is not empty. An if statement can use Python code as a condition.

The If.... Else Statement

Sometimes, you may want to generate great feedback for the user to show why something is false or any other explanation. This is the point where the ***if*** statement becomes useful. It has an extra else block that is only used when the ***if*** condition is false.
Take a look at the following example:

```
# Get two integers from the user
dividend = int(input('Please enter the number to divide: '))
divisor = int(input('Please enter dividend: '))
# If possible, divide them and report the result
if divisor != 0:
print(dividend, '/', divisor, "=", dividend/divisor)
else:
print('Division by zero is not allowed')
```

In this program, if the condition is false, the else block has a different set of code that the program runs.

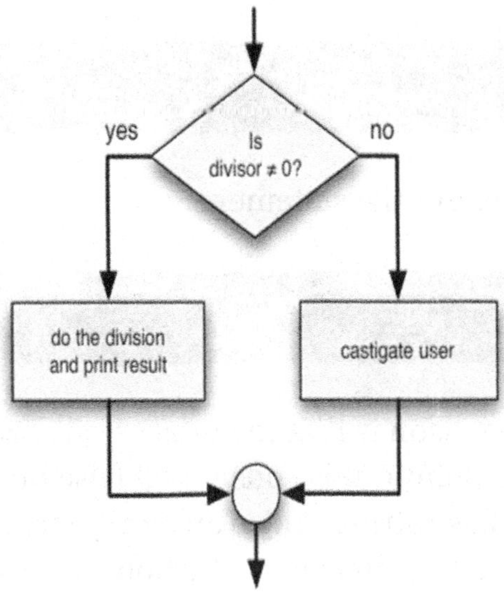

The last else block in the example highlighted notifies the user that a division by zero is not allowed. A different application can deal with the problem using a new approach like replacing a default value for the divisor rather than the zero.
The format of the if...else statement is:

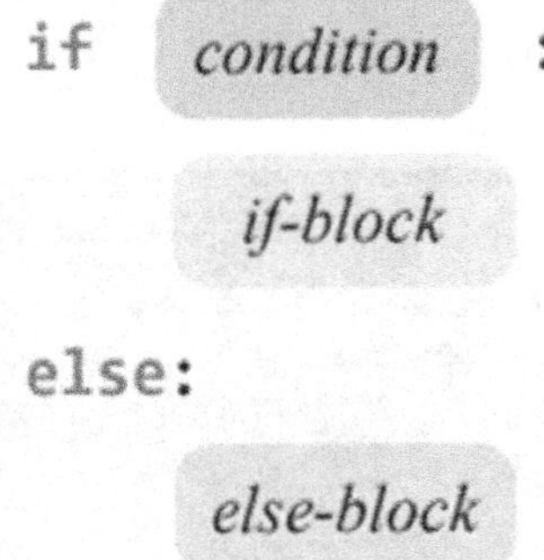

The Pass Statement

Some new engineers use the if...else statement when they could just use the if statement. For instance:

In this piece of code, if the value of the variable x is less than zero, the coder does not want to do anything. But if the number is greater than zero, the computer wants to show the value of x.

```
x = 10
if x < 0:

else:
  print(x)
```

In this program, the code should not print anything if the value of the variable x is less than 0. But this program does not work right. The else block is part of the if...else statement, but it contains no if block. The area for comments is not part of the Python statement.

Python has a unique statement called pass. The meaning of this statement is to do nothing. You can include the pass statement inside your code, in particular where you want a statement but don't want the program to execute anything. So this code snippet can be made legal using a pass statement as follows:

```
x = 10
if x < 0:
  pass  # Do nothing
else:
  print(x)
```

Even though the pass statement checks the code, a simple if statement can be used to improve its structure. When x<y is not true in math, it should be x >= y. By making the relation's truth value false inside the condition, this code can be well described as:

```
if x >= 0:
print(x)
```

So, if you want to use an empty if body in an if...else statement, you need to do the following:

1. Change the value of the condition from true to false.
2. Change the else body into the if body.
3. Get rid of the else

If you want to use an else block that does not work, do not change the condition. Instead, remove the else and else block.
In Python, it is important to use the pass statement to keep the place where the code will be written in the future. For example:

```
x = 10
if x < 0:
  pass # TODO: print an appropriate warning message to determined
else:
  print(x)
```

The programmer intends to create an if block in the following section of code, but the type of code that should go inside the if block has not been decided upon just yet. Therefore, the pass statement by acting as a stand-in for the code that is to follow. The code's notes explain more about the program.

Floating Point in Equality Operators

The task of the equality operator is to check for precise accuracy. This is a big problem when dealing with floating-point numbers because they aren't accurate.

```
d1 = 1.11 - 1.10
d2 = 2.11 - 2.10
print('d1 =', d1, ' d2 =', d2)
if d1 == d2:
print('Same')
else:
print('Different')
```

If you apply the knowledge of mathematics, the following equality should stand:

```
1.11-1.10 = 0.01 = 2.11-2.10
```

The result of the first print statement revives the perception of floating point numbers:

```
d1 = 0.010000000000000009  d2 = 0.009999999999999787
```

In this example, the expression d1==d2 determines the accuracy of the equality operator, and hence, it will indicate that the two expressions are different.
The best way to confirm whether floating-point numbers are equivalent is to look at the absolute value of the two numbers.

Nested Conditionals

Any Python function can be used inside the if, or else block. With the stacked if statement, we can make program logic as complicated as we want. For example, the following program checks to see if a number is between 0 and 10:

```
value = int(input("Please enter an integer value in the range 0...10:"))
if value >= 0:
  if value <= 10:
    print('In range')
  print('Done')
```

In this program:

- The running program first evaluates the condition. Let us say that the first value is found to be lower than zero, it will not move to the second condition, but it will shift to the next statement in the outer if.
- If the program determines that the value of the variable is greater or equivalent to the variable, it will print the statement inside the if block.

Following this line of reasoning, we have arrived at the conclusion that the first if encompasses the second if. The first "if" condition is referred to as "external," whereas the second "if" condition is referred to as "inner." It is important to keep in mind that the full if statement is located one level inward from the outer if statement. In other words, the if's block and the statement that begins ("In range") have been shifted two spaces below the statement the outer if.

Make sure you do not forget that the four-space indentation style requires four spaces to be placed between each entry in the program.

The In range message that should be written must meet both of the if block's conditions. From this point of view, the program could be rewritten with just one if statement. For example:

```
value = int(input("Please enter an integer value in the range 0...10:"))
if value >= 0 and value <= 10:
  print('In range')
print('Done')
```

This application is dependent on the user, and it checks both conditions simultaneously. The logic for this statement is simple when you use one if statement instead of an advanced Boolean expression in the condition.

The if condition in this program can be expressed in a compact manner as 0 <= value <= 10.
Sometimes, it is hard to determine the logic of a program. For example, it is impossible to rewrite the previous example using a single if statement.

```
value = int(input("Please enter an integer value in the range 0...10:"))
if value >= 0:
  if value <= 10:
    print(value, ' is in range')
  else:
    print(value, 'is too large')
else:
  print(value, 'is too small')
print('Done')
```

This program describes a specific message rather than a simple message of acceptance. Out of the three messages, at least one is displayed depending on what value is in the variable.
Binary is the format used by computers to interpret data. In contrast to the decimal number system, this format is very easy to understand. The binary system only required two digits, whereas the decimal system calls for a range of digits from 0 to 9. Even when there are no digits, no decimal integer will lack binary representation.
With the presence of 10 digits to execute, the decimal number system can tell the difference between place values and powers of 10.

Multi-Decision Statements

An easy if...else statement might pick between two approaches to achieving the same goal. This program is great to demonstrate how to choose from three options. Suppose one of the many actions should be executed.
Then you will need nested if...else statements and this page shows how nested if is used:

```
value = int(input("Please enter an integer value in the range 0...5:"))
if value < 0:
  print(value, 'is too small')
else:
  if value == 0:
    print('zero')
```

```
else:
    if value == 1:
        print('one')
    else:
        if value == 2:
            print('two')
        else:
            if value == 3:
                print('three')
            else:
                if value == 4:
                    print('four')
                else:
                    if value == 5:
                        print('five')
                    else:
                        print(value, 'is too large')
print('Done')
```

Notice the following about this program:

- Depending on what the user types in, the program will show one of the eight messages.
- Each if block has one printing line and one else block. The only if that does not have an if statement is the last one. The control code tells the program how to run so that each condition can be checked. When the first condition is met, the if body that goes with it is run. If none of the input conditions are met, the computer will show the "Too large message."

As more conditions are checked in this program, a lot of code moves to the right. Thanks to Python's if/elif/else, which is a multi-way conditional structure, programs that check a lot of conditions can be written in a way that is easy to read.

```
value = int(input("Please enter an integer value in the range 0...5:"))
if value < 0:
  print(value, 'is too small')
elif value == 0:
  print('zero')
elif value == 1:
  print('one')
elif value == 2:
```

```
  print('two')
elif value == 3:
  print('three')
elif value == 4:
  print('four')
elif value == 5:
  print('five')
else:
  print(value, 'is too large')
print('Done')
```

The words else and if were combined to form the term elif. If you are able to pronounce elif as the same as else if, then you will be able to understand how the code snippet can be modified.

When you wish to select a single block of code from a number of different possibilities, the multi-way if/elif/else statement can be of assistance. In an if/elif/else statement, the portion if is the most important part. The else clause is not required.

The if/then/elif/else syntax for statements typically looks like this:

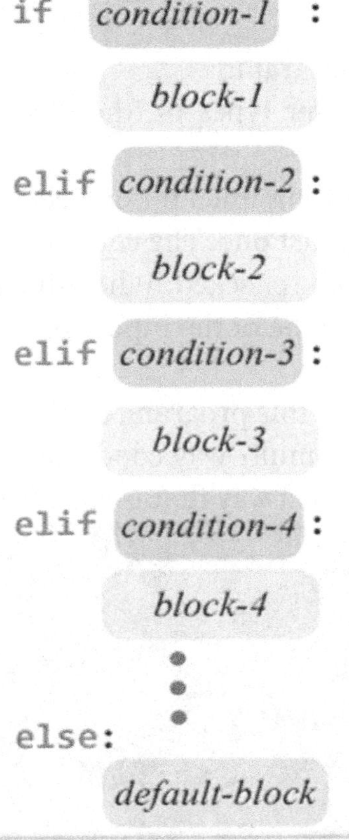

Point to remember: If an if/elif/else statement has an alternative else, only one of its blocks will be run. Which block to run is based on which of the conditions is met first. If the else block of an if/else/if/else statement is removed, the code contained in any of the other blocks can be examined to determine whether or not any of the conditions are True. Sometimes, new programmers will think that a set of simple lines is the same as a multi-way if/elif/else. If the user enters a number that is not inside the software's acceptable range, the program will not print anything; however, it will print the English term that corresponds to the number.

```
value = int(input())
if value == 0:
  print('zero')
elif value == 1:
  print('one')
elif value == 2:
  print('two')
elif value == 3:
  print('three')
elif value == 4:
  print('four')
elif value == 5:
  print('five')
print('Done')
```

Now take a look at this program. It replaces the elifs with ifs. It behaves exactly like the previous program:

```
value = int(input())
if value == 0:
  print('zero')
if value == 1:
  print('one')
if value == 2:
  print('two')
if value == 3:
  print('three')
if value == 4:
  print('four')
```

```
if value == 5:
  print('five')
print('Done')
```

Although these two programs do the same thing, the previous program is much better. Why?
The first program only performs two comparisons before making a decision and printing the message Done. On the other hand, the second program must verify each conditional expression inside the program before printing the same message. While it is hard to notice the difference, in a large complex program, the additional computation may highly affect the run time of the application. The most important thing is that it gives new coders the idea that sequential ifs is the same as multi-way if/elifs.
Examining this idea in light of the following programs should do the trick:

```
value = int(input("Enter a number:"))
if value == 1:
  print('You entered one')
elif value == 2:
  print('You entered  two')
elif value > 5:
  print('You entered a number greater than 5')
elif value == 7:
  print('You entered 7')
else:
  print('You entered some other number')
print('Done')
```

In this particular program, when a user inputs 7, the program displays the message "You entered a number greater than five."
In the second program, it converts all the elif to become ifs. This means that when a user inputs 7, the program will display the same message as in the previous example. The only difference is that this program will print an extra message that says, "You entered seven."

```
value = int(input("Enter a number:"))

if value == 1:
  print('You entered one')
if value == 2:
```

```
  print('You entered  two')
if value > 5:
  print('You entered a number greater than 5')
if value == 7:
  print('You entered 7')
else:
  print('You entered some other number')
print('Done')
```

You can observe that multi-way conditional statements act differently from sequential ifs by looking at the examples that are provided below.

Conditional Expressions

Let us look at the following code:

```
a = 10
b = 10
d = 5
e = 1
if a != b:
  c = d
else:
  c = e
```

This code will store one of the two potential values in c.

Errors Found In Conditional Statements

Examine the following compound conditional carefully:

```
value > 0 and value <= 10
```

```
value = 1

if value > 0 and value <= 10:
  print('Value between 1 .. 10')
```

One of the most common mistakes that programmers make is confusing the logical **and** and the logical **or.**
Take a look at this:

```
x > 0 or x <= 10
```

```
X = 1

if x > 0 or x <= 10:
  print('Value between 1 .. 10')
```

Which values do you think can make this expression true and also make it false? The fact is that this expression will be true regardless of what the x value is. This is an example of a tautology.
Now, assume x is a number, can you think of a number that can make the expression false? At least one of the subexpression will be true.
Programmers who use Python frequently make an error which is known as "contradiction". Assume that you do not wish to include any values that fall inside a certain range. Take, for instance, you don't want values in the range 0-10. Can this Boolean expression complete the task?

```
# All but 0, 1, 2, ..., 10
if value < 0 and value > 10:
print(value)
```

```
value = 1

# All but 0, 1, 2, ..., 10
if value < 0 and value > 10:
  print(value)
```

If you carefully examine the condition, you will learn that it cannot be true. Is there a number that can be less than zero and greater than 10 simultaneously? Of course, none. In this case, you could say that this phrase is a contradiction and a complicated way to show that it is False. To fix this piece of code, you need to change the **and** operator with **or** operator.
When it comes to operator priority, the logical or, not, and have less weight than the comparison operators. What if you want the word OK to be shown when x is 1, 2, or 3:

```
x = 1

if x == 1 or 2 or 3:
  print("OK")
```

But it does not matter what the value of x is. No matter what the value of x is, the code will always print OK. Since the == operator is more important than the or operator, Python will treat this statement as:

```
x == 1 or 2 or 3
```

This expression x == 1 can both be true or false. However, the integer 2 is considered true. Any value that evaluates to true that is contained in a chain of subexpressions that are brought together by or will cause the entire expression to evaluate to true.
The following is the proper approach to illustrate the first statement:

```
x = 1

if x == 1 or 2 or 3:
  print(x)
```

Although the Boolean expression looks verbose, that is the right way of writing Python. Keep in mind that every subexpression includes a Boolean expression but not an integer value.
In many programs, you may find programmers making small spelling error mistakes. This generally makes a program fail to run.
The keys M and N on the English keyboard are very close to each other. Therefore, it is one of the most common typographical errors that programmers make. They press N when they want to press M.
As the length of our programs increases, it can be very difficult to track down a misspelled word that causes an error in a program. Fortunately, there are tools that have been developed to help programmers deal with these kinds of challenges. Some of these Python tools include Pylint.

The Advanced Nature of Logic

There are tools available within the Python programming language that simplify the process of writing intricate conditional statements. It is of the utmost importance to avoid wanting to make things more difficult. In Boolean formulas, the employment of "or," "not," and "and" results in circumstances that are fairly difficult to understand. There is a great deal of variety in the approaches that can be taken to achieve the same goals. For instance, each and every one of these Boolean statements is equivalent.

```
a = 1
b = 1
c = 1
d = 1

print( not (a == b and c != d) )
print( not (a == b and not (c == d) ))
print( not (a == b or not (c != d) ))
print( a != b or c == d )
```

Although these expressions express the same thing, they have a different level of complexity.

Some instances demand a complex logic to attain the correct behavior of a program. However, the easiest logic that works is favorable than one, which is complex because:

- It is easy to understand simple logic.
- It is easy to write and make simple logic work because you can understand it. On the other hand, longer formulations that are somewhat more complex raise the possibility of making spelling mistakes that manifest themselves as logical flaws. These are some of the errors that are the most difficult to trace down.
- Not forgetting, a simple logic improves efficiency. Every Boolean expression and relational comparison demands a repetition in the machine. So, if you use simple logic, the entire process will be fast and efficient. For instance:

```
not (a == b and not (c == d))
```

```
a = 1
b = 1
c = 1
d = 1

print( not (a == b and not (c == d)))
```

This expression computes five different operations. In case a fails to equal b, it will only execute two operations because of something called short-circuit Boolean operation of the and. Now draw a comparison between this expression and the previous one:

```
a != b or c == d
```

```
a = 1
b = 1
c = 1
d = 1

print( a != b or c == d )
```

A running program can compute this expression faster because it consists of three computations, that being the highest. However, if a fails to equal b, the computation will short-circuit the or, and determine only the != operation.
Another reason why you need to go for simpler logic is that it is easy to change it.

Chapter 10: Iteration

In computing, the word "iteration" means to repeat the same lines of code. It is a useful programming idea that helps figure out how to solve problems. Algorithm creation is based on iteration and execution based on conditions.

While Statement

This program counts up to five and puts a number on each line of output.

```
print(1)
print(2)
print(3)
print(4)
print(5)
```

Now, how do you write code that can count to 10,000? Are you going to copy and paste the 10,000 printing lines and change them? You can, but that will get old fast. But counting is routine, and computers can count a lot of things at once. So there must be a way to do it quickly. You need to print the value of a variable and then start to add one to it. Keep doing this until you reach 10,000. Looping is the process of putting the same code in place over and over again. Python's while and for lines are the only ones that can be used to repeat something.
Here is a program that uses the while statement to count up to five:

```
count = 1 # Initialize counter
while count <= 5: # Should we continue?
print(count) # Display counter, then
count += 1 # Increment counter
```

The while statement in this program will show the variable amount over and over again. After that, this block of statements is run five times:

```
print(count)
count += 1
```

The count variable is increased by one by the software each time it is displayed in the program. After the fifth iteration, the condition will no longer be met, and as a result, the aforementioned chunk of code will no longer be executed.

```
while count <= 5:
```

This line is where the while statement starts. The condition that decides whether or not the block is run is the phrase that comes after the while keyword. As long as the outcome of the test continues to be True, the computer will proceed to execute the code block. The iteration will be terminated, however, in the event that the condition becomes false. In addition, the code block that is contained within the body of the loop will not be executed if the condition that is being checked at the beginning is found to be false.

The fundamental format of the while statement is as follows:

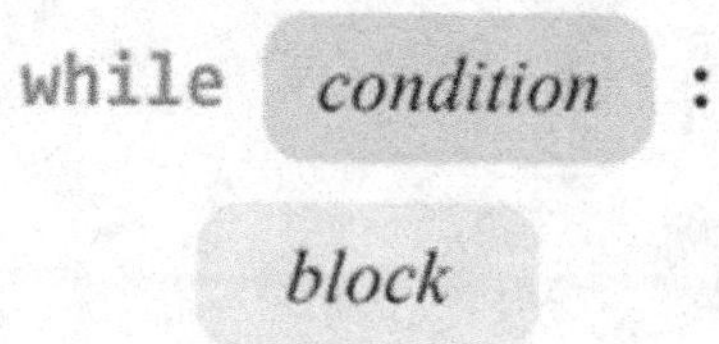

The sentence in Python starts with the reserved word while.

The body's state shows whether or not it will be executed. After the condition, there must be a colon (:).

One or more sentences that are supposed to be carried out in the event that the condition is true make up a block. It is necessary for each of the statements in the block to be moved up one level such that they are above the initial line of the while statement. Technically speaking, the block is a component of the while sentence.

As a result of the similarity in appearance between the while statement and the if statement, novice programmers may confuse the two. They might type "if" when they meant to type "while." Often, the problem is clear right away because of how different the two claims are. However, this error may be more difficult to spot in more intricate and profound logic.

The condition is checked by the currently executing program before the while block is executed. After the while block has been executed, the condition will be examined once more. If the condition continues to evaluate to "true," the code included in the while block will be executed again. If the condition is True when the program begins, it will continue to execute the block until it can be determined that the condition is no longer True. This is the moment where the loop will no longer continue to execute. This piece of software will begin counting from zero for as long as the user instructs it to do so.

```
# Counts up from zero. The user continues the count by entering 'Y'.
# The user discontinues the count by entering 'N'
count = 0  # The current count
entry = 'Y'
while entry != 'N' and entry != 'n':
  # print the current value of count
  print(count)
  entry = input('Please enter "Y" to continue or "N" to quit:')
  if entry == 'Y' or entry == 'y':
     count += 1  # Keep counting
     # Check for "bad" entry
  elif entry != 'N' or entry != 'n':
     print('"' + entry + '" is not valid choice')
```

Here is another tool where the user can type different integer that are not negative. If the user types a negative number, the computer stops taking inputs and shows the sum of all the numbers that were not negative. If the first number is a negative number, the sum will be zero.

```
sum = 0
entry = 0
print("Enter numbers to sum, negative numbers ands list:")
while entry >= 0:
  entry = int(input())
  if entry >= 0:
     sum += entry
     print(sum)
```

Let us look at how this program works:
First, there are two variables in the program: sum and entry.

- `Entry`

At the beginning, you will set the entry to 0 because we want the while statement's condition entry >= 0 to be true. In the while condition, if the variable entry has not been initialized, the program will generate an error when it attempts to perform a comparison between entry and zero. The variable record contains the user's number that was saved. Every time through the loop, the value of the variable entry changes.

- **Sum**

This is a variable that keeps the sum of all the numbers that the user has typed in. The value of this variable is initialized to zero at the start since having a value of zero indicates that it has not yet carried out any actions. If you do not set up the variable sum, the program will also throw an error when it tries to change it with the +- operator. Inside the loop, you can add the user's inputs to sum over and over again. After the loop has been completed, the sum variable will contain the total of all of the user's numbers that are not negative.

By initializing the entry to zero and checking to see if entry in the while statement is greater than or equal to zero (entry >= 0), you can ensure that the body of the while loop will only execute once. The if condition ensures that the device will never bring the sum to a negative value by adding a negative number.

If a user enters a negative number, the program that is currently running might not change the sum variable, and therefore the while condition will not be true. After the completion of the loop, the print line is executed by the program.

This program does not keep track of how many times you type an amount. But it adds up the numbers you put in the sum field.

```
print("Help! my Computer doesn't work!")
done = False
while not done:
  print("Does the computer make any sounds (fans, etc.)")
  choice = input("or show any lights? (y/n):")
  if choice == 'n':
    choice = input("Is it plugged in? (y/n):")
    if choice == 'n':
      print("Plug it in.")
    else:
      choice = input("Is the switch in the \"on\" position? (y/n):")
      if choice == 'n':
        print("Turn it on.")
      else:
        choice = input("Does the computer have a fuse? (y/n):")
        if choice == 'n':
          choice = input("Is the outlet OK? (y/n):")
          if choice == 'n':
            print("Check the outlet's circuit")
            print("breaker or fuse. Move to a ")
            print("new outlet, if necessary")
          else:
            print("Please consult a service technician.")
            done = True
        else:
          print("Check the fuse. Replace if necessary.")
  else:
    print("Please consult a service technician.")
    done = True
```

A huge amount of this program is taken up by a while block. The loop is controlled by the Boolean variable done. As long as done is while, not false, the loop will keep running. This Boolean variable's name is flag. Now, the result is true if the flag is raised, and false otherwise if not.

Do not forget that the variable *not done* is the opposite of *done*.

Definite and Indefinite Loops

Let us look at the code below:

```
n = 1
while n <= 10:
  print(n)
  n += 1
```

We examine the code and determine the appropriate number of iterations for the loop based on our findings. Because we are able to predict the exact number of times that this type of loop will occur, we refer to it as a definite loop.
Now, have a look at the code below:

```
n = 1
stop = int(input())
while n <= stop:
  print(n)
  n += 1
```

It is difficult to determine how many times it will execute based on this code alone. What the user enters affects the amount of repeats that are generated. But it is possible to know how many times the while loop will run after the user inputs something and before the next execution starts.
Because of this, the loop is called a definite loop.
Now, compare this program to the ones that came before:

```
done = False
while not done:
  entry = int(input())
  if entry == 999:
    done = True
  else:
    print(entry)
```

At no point during the running of this program's loop can you tell how many times the iterations can run. Before and after the loop, the number 999 is known, but the value of the entry can be anything the user types in. The person can stop it by putting in 0 or even 999. The while statements in this program serve as a wonderful illustration of an indefinite loop.

Therefore, the while statement is an excellent choice for loops that repeat indefinitely. Even though the while lines were used in these examples to show definite loops, Python actually has a much better way to do definite loops than using the while lines. There it is: the for element in its proper place.

The For Statement

The while loop is an excellent choice for use in loops that continue indefinitely. This has been demonstrated by the fact that you are unable to predict the amount of times the while loop will execute in the procedures that came before. In the past, the while loop was employed to execute a clear loop, such as:

```
n = 1
while n <= 10:
  print(n)
  n += 1
```

The print line will only run 10 times in the code below. To run the loop, this code needs three important parts:

- Initialization
- Check
- Update

There is a good way to show a clear loop in the Python programming language. The *for* statement is used to keep going over a list of values. A tuple is one way to show that something is in a chain. For instance:

```
for n in 1,2,3,4,5,6,7,8,9,10:
  print(n)
```

This code works just like the while loop that was shown before. In this case, the print command is executed ten times. The code will show the number 1, then the number 2, etc. The last number that comes out is 10.

It is always a pain to show all of the parts of a tuple. Think about going through all the numbers from 1 to 1,000 and writing down all the parts of the tuple. That would not make sense. Python has a quick way to show a set of numbers that all follow the same pattern. This code uses the range statement to get numbers from 1 to 10.

```
for n in range(1,11):
  print(n)
```

The for loop can assign the numbers 1, 2,....10 to the variable n by using the range object that is created when the range expression (1,11) is executed.
The meaning of the single line of code that makes up this code snippet is "for every integer n in the range of 1 to n 11." The number of times the loop is executed is equal to 1, hence the value of n within the block is one. The variable n will have a value of 2 on the subsequent round through the loop. The value of n increases by one with each iteration of the loop. The value of n will be used by the code while it is contained in the block until it reaches 10. This is how the range statement is usually put together:

range(*begin*, *end*, *step*)

From the general syntax:

- Begin is the first number in the range; when it is removed, the default value becomes 0.
- One number after the last value is the end value. This value is important, so you should not get rid of it.
- Step is the amount by which something goes up or down. If you delete step, its default number is 1.

All of the numbers for begin, step, and end must be phrases with integers. We can not use floating-point expressions or other kinds. In a range expression, the arguments can be basic numbers like 10, variables like m and n, or even more complex integer expressions..
One good thing about the range expression is that it gives you a lot of freedom. For example:

```
for n in range(21,0, -3):
  print(n, end=' ')

Output:
21 18 15 12 9 6 3
```

This means that the range can be used to show different patterns.
When there is only one input for a range expression, such as range(y), y represents the end of the range, 0 represents the starting value, and 1 represents the step value.
In expressions that take two arguments, such as range (m, n), the initial value is denoted by m, while the end value is denoted by y. The value of the step increases until it reaches 1.

In equations with three parameters, such as range (m, n, y), the start value is denoted by m, the end value is denoted by n, and the step value is denoted by y.
When using a for loop, the range object has unrestricted authority over the manner in which the loop variable is selected at each iteration.
If you take a closer look at older Python tools or even at online Python examples, you will probably run upon the xrange statement at some point. Both range and xrange are in Python version 2. But the xrange is not in Python 3. In fact, Python 3's range expression is the same as Python 2's xrange expression.
In Python 2, the range statement makes a data structure called a list. This can take some time for a program that is already working. In Python 2, the extra time is no longer needed because of the xrange statement. Because of this, it is great for a long run. Developers of Python 2 prefer to use the xrange instead of the range when making loops with the for statement. This makes the code work better.
Still, Python 3 lets you use range without changing how well it works at run time.
We suggest using the for loop because it can be used to loop over a number of integers, which is a useful and important part of making software.
Also, the for loop can go through any object that can be looped.

Nested Loops

Both while loops and for loops can have other loops inside of them. So, it is possible to put a loop inside of another loop. Take a look at the program that prints out the results of a multiplication table to see how a stacked loop works. Students of elementary level depend on the times table to master the products of integers that extend to 10 or 12.
In this part, we will write a program to do multiplication. This program will be flexible, and the user will be able to put the numbers that decide how big the table will be.
At first, only the table elements will be written. However, you will have to write a nested loop to help you display the results of the table. While that can seem tough to try out, in this first trial, the program will print only the table rows. Once it prints the rows, then we can continue to add extra features. See the program:

```
size = int(input('Please enter the tablesize: '))
for row in range(1, size+1):
  print("row #", row)
```

Output

```
Please enter the table size: 10
Row #1
Row #2
Row #3
Row #4
Row #5
Row #6
Row #7
Row #8
Row #9
Row #10
```

From the output, you can tell that it is a bit underwhelming.
This program prints rows the way we wanted—no extra details for each row.
Now, the next thing we are going to do is to add more features to the program. We want each row to have the numbers.
Here is a refined code:

```
size = int(input('Please enter the tablesize: '))
for row in range(1, size+1):
  for column in range(1, size+1):
    product = row * column
    print(product, end=' ')
  print() #Move cursor to next row
```

To show the items of each row, a loop is made. The total number of rows that the computer shows is controlled by the external loop.
What came out of the improved program:

```
Please enter the table size: 10
1 2 3 4 5 6 7 8 9 10
2 4 6 8 10 12 14 16 18 20
3 6 9 12 15 18 21 24 27 30
4 8 12 16 20 24 28 32 36 40
5 10 15 20 25 30 35 40 45 50
6 12 18 24 30 36 42 48 54 60
7 14 21 28 35 42 49 56 63 70
8 16 24 32 40 48 56 64 72 80
9 18 27 36 45 54 63 72 81 90
10 20 30 40 50 60 70 80 90 100
```

Although the numbers within each column are not well organized, they are located in the correct spots in relation to one another. Therefore, we can make the numbers align to the right by utilizing a string formatter. Here is the new code:

```
size – int(input('Please enter the tablesize: '))
for row in range(1, size+1):
  for column in range(1, size+1):
     product = row * column
     print('{0:4}'.format(product), end=' ')
  print()
```

This code makes the output to look attractive:

```
Please enter the table size: 10
   1   2   3   4   5   6   7   8   9  10
   2   4   6   8  10  12  14  16  18  20
   3   6   9  12  15  18  21  24  27  30
   4   8  12  16  20  24  28  32  36  40
   5  10  15  20  25  30  35  40  45  50
   6  12  18  24  30  36  42  48  54  60
   7  14  21  28  35  42  49  56  63  70
   8  16  24  32  40  48  56  64  72  80
   9  18  27  36  45  54  63  72  81  90
  10  20  30  40  50  60  70  80  90 100
```

Notice the presentation of the table changes based on what the user enters as input.

```
Please enter the table size: 5
   1   2   3   4   5
   2   4   6   8  10
   3   6   9  12  15
   4   8  12  16  20
   5  10  15  20  25
```

Next, let us finish this program by giving each row and column a name and adding lines around the table's edges. These changes are made with this code:

```
size = int(input('Please enter the tablesize: '))
print(" ", end=' ')
#Printing column heading
for column in range(1, size + 1):
  print('{0:4}'.format(column), end=' ')
print() # go down to the next line
```

```
print('    +', end='')

for column in range(1, size+1):
  print('----', end='')
print()

for row in range(1, size+1):
  print('{0:3}|'.format(row), end='')
  for column in range(1, size+1):
     product = row * column
     print('{0:4}'.format(product), end='')
  print()
```

The formatted output:

```
Please enter the table size: 10
        1   2   3   4   5   6   7   8   9  10
    +----------------------------------------
  1 |   1   2   3   4   5   6   7   8   9  10
  2 |   2   4   6   8  10  12  14  16  18  20
  3 |   3   6   9  12  15  18  21  24  27  30
  4 |   4   8  12  16  20  24  28  32  36  40
  5 |   5  10  15  20  25  30  35  40  45  50
  6 |   6  12  18  24  30  36  42  48  54  60
  7 |   7  14  21  28  35  42  49  56  63  70
  8 |   8  16  24  32  40  48  56  64  72  80
  9 |   9  18  27  36  45  54  63  72  81  90
 10 |  10  20  30  40  50  60  70  80  90 100
```

If a user enters 7:

```
Please enter the table size: 7
        1   2   3   4   5   6   7
    +----------------------------
  1 |   1   2   3   4   5   6   7
  2 |   2   4   6   8  10  12  14
  3 |   3   6   9  12  15  18  21
  4 |   4   8  12  16  20  24  28
  5 |   5  10  15  20  25  30  35
  6 |   6  12  18  24  30  36  42
  7 |   7  14  21  28  35  42  49
```

```
Please enter the table size: 1
        1
    +----
```

As seen, the table will change automatically depending on the input data by the user. Here is a description of how the program works:

- First, you need to tell what is done once in external loops and what is done over and over again. Look at the row headings across the top of the table. They are not contained within any of the loops. Therefore, the computer will only print it once by using a loop to do so.
- The portion of code that displays the row heads is broken up and distributed across the duration that the global loop is active. The reason for this is that it is not possible to display the heading for a row until the results for the row that comes before it have been displayed.
- The command to display the results is as follows:

```
print('{0:4}'.format(product), end='') # Display product
```

Aligns the product value to the right inside the four-character-wide field. This step will put the fields in the time's table in the right order.

- Inside the nested loop, the variable that controls the outer loop is in charge of row. The inner loop will be run by the column.
- Every single time the outer loop goes around, the inner loop does size times. In other words, the most important point is:

```
print('{0:4}'.format(product), end='')  # Display product
```

implement size x size times, once for each product in the table.

- When the program writes the information of each row, it will start a new line. So, in the inner column loop, all of the numbers are shown on the same line.

When the repetitive process needs to be done more than once, you need nested loops. The for loop shows the data of each row in the time's table, and another for loop shows each row.

Nested loops make programming more efficient, and some new programmers try to use them even when a single loop would be better. Before you use a nested loop to figure out how to solve a problem, make sure you can not solve it with a single loop. Keep in mind that stacked loops are not easy to write, and when they do not work perfectly, they are not as useful as simple loops.

Sudden Loop Termination

In general, a while loop will run until it reaches that point when the condition is false. An executing program has to check this condition first before it can implement the statements inside the body of the loop. Next, it has to run all of the lines in the loop's body before it can check the same condition again.

Even if the condition being tested is found to be false, a while loop will typically be unable to exit its body rapidly before all of the lines contained within the body have been executed. This is how the while statement works because the author may wish to run all of the lines in the body as a single block. This is one of the reasons why the while statement works this way. Despite this, there are situations in which you will need to immediately halt the body of the code or examine the state while it is still in the middle of the loop.

To put it another way, the condition of a while statement will always be verified at the very beginning of the loop by itself. It is not the case that a while loop will complete the task immediately just because the corresponding condition is met. Here's a program that shows how to exit works:

```
x = 10
while x == 10:
  print('First print statement in the while loop')
  x = 5
  print('Second print statement in the while loop')
```

Output

```
First print statement in the while loop
Second print statement in the while loop
```

Even if the condition that causes the loop to run changes inside the loop's body, the while statement can not review the condition until the loop is done to run lines inside the body. There are cases where it is better to exit a loop from the center of the loop. This means you terminate the loop before all statements within the body finish executing. In other words, if a given condition is met in the body of the loop, end the loop instantly.

The same is true when it comes to for statements. There are instances where it is necessary to terminate the for loop early. In this case, Python has a way to do that. And by applying the break statement, and continue statement, programmers have a lot of flexibility on their side.

Break Statement

As we have already said, it is sometimes important to end the loop in the middle of its body. This means you end the loop before all the lines in the body have been run. Therefore, the loop should immediately terminate whenever a particular condition is satisfied within the body of the loop. It is possible, but not necessary, for the "middle-exiting" condition to be the same requirement that directs the while loop.

The break line in Python is utilized when running code that leaves a loop in the middle of its execution. The break statement modifies the manner that the break statement is executed, making it so that it exits the body of the loop instantly. The following program shows how the break line can be used:

```
entry = 0
sum = 0

print("Enter numbers to sum, negative number ands list:")
while True:
  entry = int(input())
  if entry < 0:
    break
  sum += entry
  print('Sum:', sum)
```

The condition of the ***while*** statement will always be true. Therefore, when the program executes, it is a must for it to start to implement the statements inside the ***while*** block at least once.

Because the ***while*** sentence condition is guaranteed to be met at all times, the ***break*** line is the only way to successfully exit the while loop. In this particular scenario, the break statement will not take effect until after it determines whether or not the user entered a negative value. If the program runs into a break statement while it is being executed, it will immediately terminate the loop without reading any of the lines that are located after the main body of the loop.

The word ***break*** is reserved, so it means "break out of the loop." In the earlier case, it is hard to add a negative number to the variable sum because of where the break statement is.

Some designers of software tell programmers to use the break line in their programs as little as possible because it changes the regular way loops are controlled. Most of the time, each loop should only have one place to enter and one place to leave.

Still, some developers put the ***break*** statements inside the ***while*** statements when the condition for a ***while*** is not a tautology. By adding a break line to this loop, you can make a second way out. Many programmers think it is fine to have two exit points, but having two break points in a single loop is not a good idea, and you should avoid it.

In a while loop, you do not need the break line to have full control. In other words, you can change a Python program with a break statement inside a while loop to work the same way as one that does not have a ***break*** statement.

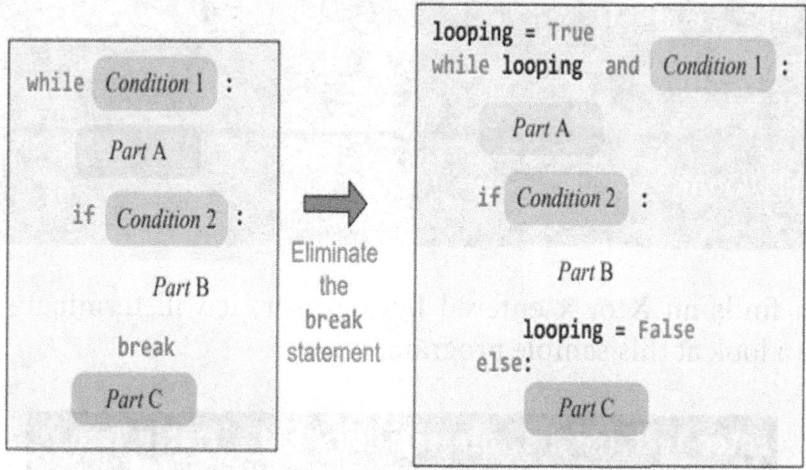

The left code illustrates a "while loop" that includes a "break statement." Towards the right, the loop is converted into a function equivalent that doesn't apply a break statement.

When you don't use a break version, then you have to consider the Boolean variable and the advanced state of the logic control loop. Also, this program without a break statement has additional overheads. For instance, it will consume more time and memory. However, the extra overhead is invisible. Even when it is insignificant, you need to note that it is more difficult to write this particular code. That is why a simple break statement can be a better control option.

Additionally, it is possible to include a break statement within a ***for*** loop. Here is an example of how you can let a break statement end a for loop.

```
word = input('Enter text (noX\'s, please): ')
vowel_count = 0
for c in word:
  if c == 'A' or c == 'a' or \
      c == 'E' or c == 'c' or \
      c == 'I' or c == 'i' or \
      c == 'O' or c == 'o' or \
      c == 'U' or c == 'u':
    print(c, ', ', sep='', end='')
    vowel_count += 1
  elif c == 'X' or c == 'x':
    break
  print(' (', vowel_count, ' vowels)', sep='')
```

If the program finds an X or x entered by the user, it will terminate from the loop suddenly. Take a look at this sample program.

```
Enter text (no X's, please): Mary had a lixtle lamb.
a, a, a, i,  (4 vowels)
```

This program will exit from the loop when it tries to execute x.

The ***break*** statement is crucial when instances arise that demand quick termination of the loop. In Python language, the ***for*** loop will function differently from the way a ***while*** loop operates. The ***for*** loop doesn't have an explicit condition that it verifies to proceed with the execution. If you want to leave a ***for*** loop early, before it has finished iterating, you have to use a break statement. The ***for*** loop is a set loop. In this case, the number of times the loop will run can be predicted by the coder. This can be changed with the ***break*** statement. As a result, programmers prefer to use a break statement in place of ***for*** loops less often.

Continue Statement

When the code of a program encounters a break statement while it is iterating through a loop, it skips the remaining instructions contained within the loop's body and terminates the iteration.

The only thing that differentiates the ***continue*** statement from the break statement is that the continue statement does not actually terminate the loop like the break statement does.

The ***continue*** statement bypasses the rest of the code included within the loop's body and immediately verifies whether or not the condition of the loop has been met. If the condition of the loop evaluates to "true," the program will restart at the beginning of the loop. This program demonstrates a ***continue*** statement in operation:

```
sum = 0
done = False
while not done:
  val = int(input('Enter positive integer (999 quits):'))
  if val < 0:
    print("Negative value", val, "ignored")
    continue
  if val != 999:
    print("Tallying", val)
    sum += val
  else:
    done = (val == 999)
    print("Sum= ", sum)
```

Because it is simple to convert code that contains a continue statement into code that does not contain one, many programmers do not utilize the continue statement in the same manner that they utilize the break statement. There is no continue line in the code shown below:

```
sum = 0
done = False
while not done:
  val = int(input('Enter positive integer (999 quits):'))
  if val < 0:
    print("Negative value", val, "ignored")
  else:
    if val != 999:
      print("Tallying", val)
      sum += val
    else:
      done = (val == 999)
      print("Sum= ", sum)
```

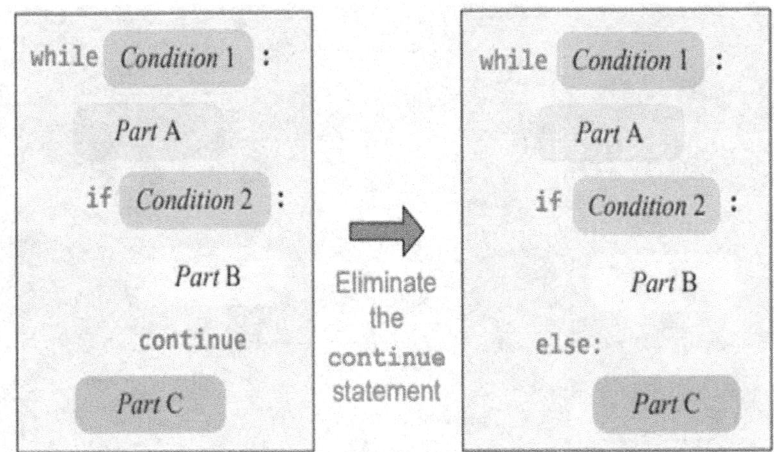

Any loop that includes the continue statement is in the code on the left. If you take out the continue statement, you can change the code on the left. The number on the right shows this.

Compared to a break statement, this change is very simple. The reason for this is that the condition of the loop stays the same and there is no need for an extra variable. The logic used in the else version is not any more sophisticated than the logic used in the continue version. In contrast to the break statement, which we discussed earlier, the continue statement never has a valid justification for its use. Sometimes, in order to address a special scenario that was overlooked, a developer will wait until the very end of the process to add a continue statement. If the body of the loop is going to be quite lengthy, the programmer can add a conditional statement and a "continue" at the very beginning of the body without having to worry about the logic of the remaining portions of the loop.

Since this is the case, the continue statement is an excellent option for the programmer to go with.

While/Else & For/Else

The iteration process in Python can support an additional ***else*** block. When the loop terminates in the typical manner, the code in the else block, which is also in the form of a loop, is executed. To put it another way, if the loop ends because of a ***break*** statement, the code in the else block does not run.

When a while loop ends because the standard check shows that the condition is false, the else block is put into place. This holds true regardless of whether the condition is discovered to be true or untrue before the body has had a chance to execute the test. This program demonstrates the way a while/else statement operates:

```
count = sum = 0
print('Please provide five non negative numbers when prompted')
while count < 5:
  val = float(input('Enter number:'))
  if val < 0:
    print('Negative numbers not acceptable! Terminating')
    break
  else:
    count += 1
    sum += val
print('Average = ', sum/count)
```

In this program, once the user enters only nonnegative values, the program will evaluate the average of the entered values.

If the user does not follow the directions, the program will show a warning saying what to do, but it will not try to figure out what the average is.

```
Please provide five nonnegative numbers when prompted
Enter number: 23
Enter number: 12
Enter number: 14
Enter number: 10
Enter number: 11
Average = 14.0
```

It could make sense to interpret the else part of the while statement as "if no break," which would indicate to execute the code in the else block only if the programme did not reach the break statement while it was operating in the while unit.
It does not matter about the else block. This program applies the if...else statement to accomplish the same effect.

```
count = sum = 0
print('Please provide five non negative numbers when prompted')
while count < 5:
  val = float(input('Enter number:'))
  if val < 0:
    break
  count += 1
  sum += val
  if count < 5:
    print('Negative numbers not acceptable! Terminating')
  else:
    print('Average = ', sum / count)
```

The while/else statement is the same as a for statement followed by an else block. When this line ends because it has found all of the numbers in a range or all of the characters in a string, the code in the connected else block is run. If a for...else block ends too soon because it runs into a break line, the code in the else block will not be run. The following program illustrates how for...else works:

```
word = input('Enter text (noX\'s, please): ')
vowel_count = 0
for c in word:
 if c == 'A' or c == 'a' or \
      c == 'E' or c == 'e' or \
      c == 'I' or c == 'i' or \
      c == 'O' or c == 'o' or \
      c == 'U' or c == 'u':
   print(c, ', ', sep='', end='')
   vowel_count += 1
 elif c == 'X' or c == 'x':
   print('X not allowed')
   break
 print(' (', vowel_count, ' vowels)', sep='')
```

Infinite Loops

For new programmers, infinite loop refers to one that runs a block of statements iteratively until the user forces the program to stop. As long as the program changes to thc body of the loop, it can not get out.

Some things are made to have endless loops on purpose. For example, a program that runs on a server for a long time, like the web server, may need to check every time for new links. This process can be done by the web server using a loop that runs forever. Beginners should learn about a planned endless loop. When new writers are coding, they often make mistakes that lead to logic errors in their programs.

For example:

```
while True:
# Do something forever. . .
```

```
while True:
  print('Hello')
```

In this code fragment, the Boolean Literal True will be true forever. So the only way to terminate the loop is to use a break statement. It is easy to create deliberate infinite loops. However, accidental infinite loops are very popular but can be a huge mountain to climb for new developers.

To avoid creating infinite loops, you need to make sure that the loop contains specific features:

- The condition of the loop should not be a tautology. For example:

```
while i >= 1 or i <= 10:
# Block of code follows ...
```

```
i = 5
while i >= 1 or i <= 10:
  print('Hello')
```

The above statement will make an infinite loop because the condition will be met by any number for i. Most likely, the coder meant to use ***and*** instead of ***or*** to stay in the loop if i is between 1 and 10.

- The while condition needs to be met in order to access its body at the beginning. The code that is contained within the body needs to make a specific modification to the state of the programme in order for it to be able to alter the outcome of the condition that is satisfied each time. This indicates that the body must always make some sort of adjustment to one of the variables. The loop ends when the variable is given a number that makes the condition no longer true.

Chapter 11: Tips to Learn Python Programming

We are happy that you have made up your mind to start the journey of mastering Python. One of the most common questions that new learners want to know is how to learn a given language.
Well, the first step in becoming a master in Python programming is to ensure that you know how to learn. Knowing how to learn is a vital skill in computer programming.
Why is it important for you to know how to learn? Simply put: language changes, new libraries are created, and new tools are released. Thus, if you know how to learn, it will be important to help you remain at par with these changes and become a successful developer.
This chapter will provide you with tips that will help you kick start your journey of becoming a master in python programming.

How to Make New Concepts Stick

Practice coding daily

Consistency is a key element when trying to learn anything new. Whether you want to learn how to drive a car, how to cook pizza, or even play basketball, you must be consistent. And learning a new language isn't an exception. You may not believe it but muscle memory plays a huge role in programming. By coding daily, you will be boosting that muscle memory. Although this can be difficult in the first few weeks, you should try and begin with 25 minutes per day, and slowly increase the length of time each day.

Write something down

Concepts will not stick in your brain just by staring at them; you must have a pen and a notebook to take notes. Research indicates that taking notes by hand increases the level of retention. If you want to become a full-time Python developer, then you must take notes, and write down some lines of code.
When you are just beginning to work on smaller programmes, writing them out by hand can be an effective way to plan your code before you move to working on the computer. This will save you a significant amount of time, particularly if you are able to make a list of the classes, variables, and methods that you will want.

Don't be dull but be active

Whether you are learning how to debug an application or learning about Python lists, the Python shell should be your favorite tool. Use it to test out some Python codes and concepts.

Give yourself a break

You know that work without play makes Jack a dull boy, so take breaks and allow the concepts to sink. Take a break of 25 minutes, then come back and resume your learning process. Breaks ensure that you have an efficient study session, especially when you are learning new information.

Breaks will be crucial when you start to debug your program. If you get a bug and you can't tell how to fix it, a break could answer your problem. Step away from your computer and refresh yourself.

Maybe it could be a missing quotation mark that is preventing your program from running, and that break will make a difference.

Love to fix bugs

When it comes to hitting bugs, this is one thing that you will never miss if you begin to write advanced Python programs. Running into bugs is something that happens to everyone who codes. It doesn't matter which language you are using. Don't let bugs get the better of you. So you need to embrace any moment you encounter a bug and think of yourself as a master of solving bugs.

When you start to debug, ensure that you have a methodological strategy to assist you in identifying where things are going wrong. Scanning through your code by following the steps in which the program is implemented is a great way to debug. Once you identify the problem, then you can think of how to solve it.

Work with others

Surround yourself with people who are learning

While coding can appear as a solitary task, it really works well when you collaborate with others. It is very crucial that when you are learning how to program in Python that you have friends who are in the same boat as you. This will give you room to share amongst yourselves the tricks to help in learning.

Don't be scared if you don't have anyone that you can collaborate with. In fact, there are many ways to meet like-minded developers passionate about Python development. You can go to local events and peer to peer learning communities for Python lovers and Meetups.

Teach

The best way to master something is to teach others. This is true when you are learning Python. There are different ways you can do this. For example, you can create blog posts that describe newly learned concepts, record videos where you explain something, or even talk to yourself. Each of these methods will solidify your knowledge and reveal any gaps in your understanding.

Try out pair programming

In this approach, two programmers work in a single workstation to finish a task. The two developers then switch tasks. One writes the code and the other one guides the process and reviews the code as it is being written. Switch tasks often to experience the benefit of both sides.

This technique has many advantages. For instance, you get the chance to have another person review your code and also see how the other person could be thinking about the problem. Getting exposed to numerous ideas and approaches of thinking will help you know how to create solutions to problems using Python.

Ask smart questions

You may have heard someone say that there is no bad question but in programming, it is possible to ask a bad question. When asking questions from someone who has very little knowledge or context of the problem you want to solve, it is advised to follow this format:

G: Give context on the area you want to solve.

O: Outline everything you have attempted to fix

O: Offer the best guess of what the problem could be.

D: Demonstrate what is happening

Asking a good question can save a lot of time. If you skip any of the following steps can lead to conflict because of the back-and-forth conversations. As a new programmer, you want to ensure that you only ask good questions so that you can learn how to express your thought process. Also, the people who help you can be happy to assist you again.

Create something

Above all, you only learn by doing. Doing exercises will help you make important steps but building something will take you far.

Build anything

For new beginners, there are always small exercises that will boost your confidence in Python. Once you have a solid foundation on basic data structures, writing classes, and object-oriented programming, then you can begin to build something.

What you build is not as important as the method you use. The path of the building is what will help you learn the most. You can only learn a lot from reading Python books, articles, and courses. Most of your learning will originate from developing something. The problems you will solve will help you learn a lot.

If you find it hard to come up with a python practice project to work on, you can get started with the following:

- Dice roll simulator.
- Number guessing game.
- Simple calculator.
- Bitcoin price notification system

Participate in open source programs

In the open source system, you can access the source code of a software, and anyone can take part. Python has a lot of open-source projects that you can decide to contribute to. Besides that, many companies post open-source projects, you can contribute to the code written and generated by engineers working in some of these companies.

Conclusion

We have covered the basics of the Python programming language. The constructs we have learned so far, such as loops, expressions, and conditions, should help you further your career in Python development.

Although not everything has been covered, what we have covered is enough to help you understand Python examples. We have tried to provide you with a refresher in Python that you can build on to become an excellent programmer. Python is one of the top four widely used programming languages. As it has increased in popularity, its main focus on the quality of code and readability, as well as the associated impact on developer productivity, appears to have been the driving force to Python success.

If you experience difficulties with some of the concepts discussed in this book, it is good if you can explore other introductory resources to help you understand. You can even consult with an experienced Python developer.

In general, you should try to master the basics of Python discussed inside this book, the language syntax, and then start to deepen your knowledge on specific features of Python. Keep in mind that great programmers don't stop learning. So make a point always to learn something new in Python every day.

Made in the USA
Monee, IL
16 November 2023